Silent Refuge

THE AZRIELI SERIES OF HOLOCAUST SURVIVOR MEMOIRS: PUBLISHED TITLES

Silent Refuge

Margrit Rosenberg Stenge

THE AZRIELI FOUNDATION
www.azrielifoundation.org

Cover and book design by Mark Goldstein
Endpaper maps by Martin Gilbert
Map on page xxix by François Blanc

LIBRARY AND ARCHIVES CANADA CATALOGUING IN PUBLICATION

Rosenberg Stenge, Margrit, author
    Silent Refuge / Margrit Rosenberg Stenge.

(Azrieli series of Holocaust survivor memoirs. Series IX)
ISBN 978-1-988065-19-9 (softcover)

1. Rosenberg Stenge, Margrit. 2. Holocaust, Jewish (1939–1945) — Germany — Personal narratives. 3. Holocaust, Jewish (1939–1945) — Norway — Personal narratives. 4. Jewish children in the Holocaust — Germany — Biography. 5. Jewish children in the Holocaust — Norway — Biography. 6. Holocaust survivors — Sweden — Biography. 7. Holocaust survivors — Canada — Biography. I. Title.

DS134.42.R66A3 2017   940.53'18092   C2017-903708-0

PRINTED IN CANADA

The Azrieli Series of Holocaust Survivor Memoirs

Naomi Azrieli, Publisher

Jody Spiegel, Program Director
Arielle Berger, Managing Editor
Farla Klaiman, Editor
Matt Carrington, Editor
Elizabeth Lasserre, Senior Editor, French-Language Editions
Elin Beaumont, Senior Education Outreach and Program Facilitator
Catherine Person, Educational Outreach and Events Coordinator,
    Quebec and French Canada
Stephanie Corazza, Education and Curriculum Associate
Marc-Olivier Cloutier, Educational Outreach and Events Assistant,
    Quebec and French Canada
Tim MacKay, Digital Platform Manager
Elizabeth Banks, Digital Asset Curator and Archivist
Susan Roitman, Office Manager (Toronto)
Mary Mellas, Executive Assistant and Human Resources (Montreal)

Mark Goldstein, Art Director
François Blanc, Cartographer
Bruno Paradis, Layout, French-Language Editions

Contents

Series Preface:
In their own words. . .

In telling these stories, the writers have liberated themselves. For so many years we did not speak about it, even when we became free people living in a free society. Now, when at last we are writing about what happened to us in this dark period of history, knowing that our stories will be read and live on, it is possible for us to feel truly free. These unique historical documents put a face on what was lost, and allow readers to grasp the enormity of what happened to six million Jews — one story at a time.

David J. Azrieli, C.M., C.Q., M.Arch
Holocaust survivor and founder, The Azrieli Foundation

Since the end of World War II, over 30,000 Jewish Holocaust survivors have immigrated to Canada. Who they are, where they came from, what they experienced and how they built new lives for themselves and their families are important parts of our Canadian heritage. The Azrieli Foundation's Holocaust Survivor Memoirs Program was established to preserve and share the memoirs written by those who survived the twentieth-century Nazi genocide of the Jews of Europe and later made their way to Canada. The program is guided by the conviction that each survivor of the Holocaust has a remarkable story to tell, and that such stories play an important role in education about tolerance and diversity.

Millions of individual stories are lost to us forever. By preserving the stories written by survivors and making them widely available to a broad audience, the Azrieli Foundation's Holocaust Survivor Memoirs Program seeks to sustain the memory of all those who perished at the hands of hatred, abetted by indifference and apathy. The personal accounts of those who survived against all odds are as different as the people who wrote them, but all demonstrate the courage, strength, wit and luck that it took to prevail and survive in such terrible adversity. The memoirs are also moving tributes to people — strangers and friends — who risked their lives to help others, and who, through acts of kindness and decency in the darkest of moments, frequently helped the persecuted maintain faith in humanity and courage to endure. These accounts offer inspiration to all, as does the survivors' desire to share their experiences so that new generations can learn from them.

The Holocaust Survivor Memoirs Program collects, archives and publishes these distinctive records and the print editions are available free of charge to educational institutions and Holocaust-education programs across Canada. They are also available for sale to the general public at bookstores. All revenues to the Azrieli Foundation from the sales of the Azrieli Series of Holocaust Survivor Memoirs go toward the publishing and educational work of the memoirs program.

~

The Azrieli Foundation would like to express appreciation to the following people for their invaluable efforts in producing this book: Doris Bergen, Sherry Dodson (Maracle Inc), Barbara Kamieński, Karen Kligman, Therese Parent, and Margie Wolfe and Emma Rodgers of Second Story Press.

About the Glossary

The following memoir contains a number of terms, concepts and historical references that may be unfamiliar to the reader. For information on major organizations; significant historical events and people; geographical locations; religious and cultural terms; and foreign-language words and expressions that will help give context and background to the events described in the text, please see the glossary beginning on page 207.

Introduction

Margrit Rosenberg Stenge's memoir, *Silent Refuge*, finds its place within the much larger story of Holocaust memory. Arriving in Canada in 1951, she and her husband are two of the close to 40,000 Jews who found post-war refuge in Canada.[1]

The story of the Holocaust is now quite a prominent part of our culture. Impressive institutions devote themselves to Holocaust memory, institutions such as the United States Holocaust Memorial Museum in Washington, DC, or Yad Vashem in Jerusalem, Israel. Even in Berlin, the city where Germans planned and instigated the horrors of the Holocaust, there is both a Holocaust memorial and a Jewish museum with exhibits that highlight the history of the Holocaust. Narratives of the Holocaust have also become a part of popular culture, starting with Steven Spielberg's 1993 film, *Schindler's List*.

It was not always so. In the first decades after Nazi Germany collapsed in 1945, Jewish survivors rarely talked about their experiences. This silence was at least partially self-protective, as they tried to stifle recurring nightmares or other symptoms of post-traumatic stress. Additionally, however, survivors often discovered that many people did not want to hear their horrific stories, or, worse yet, did not fully believe them.[2] This disinterest and skepticism was seen even among those who might have been considered a sympathetic audience. For example, one of the three dozen survivors of the death camp at Sobibor, Thomas Blatt, tried to tell his story in Israel in the late 1950s.

Hoping to find a publisher for his memoir, he was told he must have "a tremendous imagination."[3] His story about Sobibor, the death camp where 250,000 Jews were murdered and where a mass break-out occurred in 1943, was virtually unknown and had to wait until the 1980s to find an audience. *Escape from Sobibor*, a book by Richard Rashke, finally told the story in 1982.[4] *Escape from Sobibor* then became a BBC-produced film in 1987, starring Alan Arkin and Rutger Hauer among others. Thomas Blatt assisted in the creation of that film. Finally, in 1997, Blatt was able to publish his own memoir, *From the Ashes of Sobibor*.

Awareness of the Holocaust did not begin in the 1980s, of course. Newspaper stories appeared even as the Nazi persecution of Jews was taking place.[5] Anyone paying attention knew of Hitler's antisemitism as he came to power in January of 1933. They could follow the story as German laws placed harsher and harsher restrictions on the 500,000 Jews living in and fleeing Germany over the next few years. These were the sort of restrictions that pushed Margrit Stenge and her parents, plus about 300,000 other Jews, out of Germany by the end of 1939. After Germany started World War II by invading Poland on September 1, 1939, stories about the brutal mistreatment of Central- and Eastern-European Jews made it into news stories in the west. When the widespread, methodical murder of Jews began in 1941, some portions of this secret but shocking story even got reported.[6] Finally, in the summer of 1945, the story burst upon the pages of newspapers and magazines when photojournalists such as Lee Miller and Margaret Bourke-White followed Allied troops to camps such as Dachau, Buchenwald and Mauthausen. After years of rumours and partially buried press reports on horrible conditions and mass murder, this physical evidence shocked Allied troops. When photojournalists placed their photos in publications such as *Life* magazine, the images shocked the world. The first of the Nuremberg Trials, held from November 1945 until October 1946, then received considerable news coverage and added to the body of evidence available to observers.

Despite the enormity of this story, awareness of the Holocaust

receded after the war. This near disappearance of Holocaust memory was rectified first by historians. The enterprising scholarship of
historians such as Raul Hilberg, whose book *The Destruction of the
European Jews* appeared in 1961, and Christopher Browning, who,
along with many other critical works, published his path-breaking
study, *Ordinary Men: Reserve Police Battalion 101 and the Holocaust
in Poland* in 1998, created what is now known as the field of Holocaust Studies. Since the beginning of Hilberg's work in the 1950s, and
Browning's in the 1970s, the number of Holocaust scholars has grown
extensively. While historians followed the lead of Hilberg and Browning, adding to our store of Holocaust memory, scholars in literature,
religion, psychology, political science, sociology, art and other fields
studied the Holocaust through their own lenses. Together these individuals have built our scholarly foundation for Holocaust memory.
There is another essential source for Holocaust memory, however:
people like Margrit Rosenberg Stenge who personally remember it.
She and many others can tell us about the Holocaust because they are
the ones who experienced it.

Personal Holocaust testimony began to expand in the 1980s, at
about the same time Holocaust scholarship was beginning to take off.
By that time, Holocaust survivors were more likely to speak only to
their children and grandchildren. But many also started telling their
stories at schools, libraries, synagogues and churches. I have been
teaching college-level courses in the Holocaust since the late 1970s,
and my students have regularly described the visit of a Holocaust
survivor as a highlight of the course. The courage and willingness of
survivors to tell their stories in person is a particularly human and
effective way to make this horrendous story real, especially for generations born after 1945.

～

Silent Refuge gives us one very specific story of the Holocaust and
its effect on individuals. Six million Jews were murdered. Margrit
Stenge suffered the loss of both her maternal grandparents, sent to

Theresienstadt and then murdered in Auschwitz. Her father's sister Karolienchen (as Margrit called her) and her husband, Natan, were sent to live in a Jewish house in Cologne and then deported to Nazi-occupied Riga, where they died. Her father's sister Selma, along with her husband, were deported and murdered as well. That means six close family members were among the six million dead. Margrit and her parents were among the more fortunate ones, since they survived. They were also lucky in their comfortable start in life, given her father's successful business, their beautiful and impressive house in Cologne and the servants who watched over Margrit and handled most household tasks for Margrit's mother. All of these extra advantages, along with some good timing and good fortune, helped Margrit and her parents survive the Holocaust, but their survival was often frightening, and sometimes very dangerous.

Born in Germany in late December 1928, Margrit turned four years old one month before Hitler and the Nazi Party rose to power. Her father's onset of ill health seemed far more serious to her than the political change, of which she was mostly unaware. At the age of seven, however, in her second school year, she was forced to attend a Jewish school. The following year, young German children threw rocks at her in what should have been the shelter of her own walled garden. Only her father's arrival frightened them away. That incident ended her freedom to leave their home without a nanny or parent to protect her. In 1937, while visiting family where her father had grown up, a mob spent hours throwing stones at the house and breaking windows. This small mob foreshadowed the nationwide attack on plate glass windows, shops, homes and synagogues in November 1938, the "November Pogrom," also called Kristallnacht. Even before the mob violence of Kristallnacht, Margrit's parents had seen enough and decided they had to flee. Fortunately, her father's business connections and resources made this possible.

Margrit and her parents were among the approximately 300,000 Jews who fled Germany before the worst of the persecution and the final policy of murder set in. However, they were also among those

Jews not able to flee far enough, and so they remained in danger. Their first stop was in Brussels in September 1938. Margrit then spent three months with another German-Jewish refugee family in Brussels while her parents travelled to Denmark and Sweden. Finally, her father found a company in Norway interested in his Cologne company's paint formulas, which he had managed to bring with him from Germany. Margrit and her parents settled in Oslo by January 1939, gradually learning the language and increasing their comfort level in this new city. Their new life in Norway meant changing from a grand house in Cologne to a small apartment in Oslo. It also meant that Margrit's mother had to take on household tasks to which she was not accustomed. However, they were safe, comfortable and making new friends, especially among the Jewish community in Norway.

On the night of April 8, 1940, the Germans invaded Norway, ending the Rosenberg family's brief period of comfort. Margrit's father, anticipating the invasion, had already begun arranging their escape from Oslo. Early the next morning, a Norwegian from Mr. Rosenberg's paint factory picked them up in a small car and drove them two hours out of Oslo to a country inn. There they felt the need to explain their German accents, so they admitted they were Jewish refugees now in need of shelter. The next day they travelled all day "on a truck, a milk wagon and a horse and carriage" to a remote village. Someone in the inn had thought a particular electrician and his wife in that village would have a room to rent, which proved true.

Although the Rosenbergs fled Oslo with almost no extra food, clothing or money, this was an escape that saved their lives. Jews in Oslo and other Norwegian cities immediately began suffering in 1940 and 1941. In November 1942, nearly 530 Jews were placed on a German ship, the *Donau*. They were transported to Auschwitz, where only two dozen survived. In the tiny village of Rogne, where the Rosenbergs had arrived, the village policeman assured them that he would not turn them in, nor would their neighbours. Even though he later joined the Nazi Party (the *Nasjonal Samling* in Norway) — to keep a "real" Nazi from being put in the job, he said — he stayed true to his word.

The experience of Margrit and her family during their escape to remote Norway was neither comfortable nor lacking in danger. During their first two days, before the Norwegian capitulation, they were shot at by German planes. Then, to avoid the need for identification papers, they spent the summers of 1940 and 1941 at a remote cabin in the mountains. Though the setting was lovely, they had no electricity, had to fetch water from a brook and chopped their own firewood. In March 1942, due to the threat of a German police raid, they were encouraged by their local policeman to flee to that mountain cabin, despite the treacherous winter weather. Fleeing in the winter meant hours of travel on cross-country skis to get there, followed by struggles with ice and mounds of snow impeding all of their daily tasks.

During the fall of 1942, Margrit and her family heard the news of the nearly eight hundred Jews who were being rounded up and shipped from Norway to Germany, which, of course, really meant being shipped to their deaths at Auschwitz. Members of the Norwegian Underground responded to this danger by helping Jews escape to Sweden. During the summer of 1941 at their mountain cabin, the Rosenbergs had met a young law student named Einar Wellén. They saw him again in the summer of 1942, and he suggested that he contact a friend in the Underground to help them escape Nazi-occupied Norway.

In January 1943, Einar Wellén and his friend, Arne Myrvold, knocked on the Rosenbergs' door in the outskirts of Rogne. They had travelled all night on an open truck bed to announce an escape plan. It involved leaving the next morning and travelling by truck and train to a barn near Oslo. Then they would be packed on the bed of a truck with about thirty others, covered by a tarpaulin weighted down by grass. They were brought near the Swedish border, then walked quietly through the snowy night until they heard: "Welcome to Sweden."

∼

As we learn about the specific life of Margrit Rosenberg Stenge, we also learn something about the four main settings where her life took place. It is tempting to draw national stereotypes. In this particular story, the actions of Germans are violent and hateful. Norwegians, Swedes and Canadians are shown to be much more welcoming and helpful. We must search for lessons when we examine a historical episode as horrific as the Holocaust. The murder of six million Jews and about five million other Holocaust victims represents an almost unbelievable catastrophe and also a warning.[7] The world has rightly learned to condemn this event,[8] and a close look at the life of Margrit Rosenberg Stenge teaches us a particular part of this history. It also teaches us that attempts to assess national character are complicated.

For example, the Rosenbergs considered themselves good Germans. Margrit's father earned an Iron Cross for bravery fighting for Germany in World War I. He thought that his Jewish family would not be in danger under the Nazis, since their roots in Germany went back to the sixteenth century. Margrit mentions her fondness for German songs and her continuing commitment to certain German values, like organization and hard work. In the second half of the nineteenth century and first decades of the twentieth century, many Jews throughout Europe shared this positive view of Germany held by the Rosenbergs. Large numbers of them moved to Germany for a better life. Germany, at that time, promised better legal protection for Jews, better educational options, greater economic opportunity, and a less virulent antisemitism than could be found in Russia or in the Polish or Ukrainian portions of the Austrian Empire. Many Jewish families found great success in Germany, whether newly arrived or, like Margrit's family, having enjoyed centuries of residence. One of the other features of this German-Jewish symbiosis can be found in some of the greatest geniuses produced by Germany, individuals such as Albert Einstein.

Another complicated feature of Jewish life in Germany involved the partial loss of Jewish identity. As one sees in this memoir, German

Jews were far more likely to be secular than the mostly Orthodox, Yiddish-speaking Jews growing up in an Eastern European shtetl. German Jews were often more likely to identify first as German, rather than as Jewish. Ironically, these German Jews, with their great longing to be German, were the first Jews of Europe to come under the iron boot of Nazi antisemitism. It also might seem ironic that the suffering of Jews tended to nurture rather than destroy their pride in being Jewish. Margrit's sense of being Jewish certainly increased a great deal as she suffered persecution. It is common to find the children and grandchildren of Holocaust survivors being more religious than their parents or more likely, perhaps, to move to Israel.

This complicated relationship of Jews to Germany does not necessarily mean approval of Germans or the loss of antagonism. Some survivors would never buy a Volkswagen or set foot on German soil. Others, however, are willing to return to Germany, as Margrit has done, and, fortunately, many Germans now acknowledge their guilt and show respect for the Jews whose lives and families were destroyed. One example of this respect is the commemorative stones that Margrit describes in the epilogue of her memoir. These "Stolpersteine" (sometimes called "stumble stones") set in sidewalks publicly acknowledge the homes where Jews lived before being gathered up and sent off to their deaths, or at least forced to flee.

It is important to recognize that Jewish families such as the Rosenbergs appreciated their German identity. It also is important to note the crisis atmosphere suffered by Germans in the years leading up to the rise of Hitler. They lost World War I. Two million Germans died in that war. They suffered the loss of big chunks of German territory and they were told they had to pay huge reparations for war damage. Then they experienced a crisis of hyper-inflation in 1922 to 1923 and the Great Depression from 1930 to 1933. These multiple crises help explain why Germans were willing to turn to a leader as radical as Adolf Hitler.

Germans made some extremely poor decisions in their response to the crises of the 1920s. As one historian has written, "It should be stated clearly that Germans became Nazis because they wanted to become Nazis and because the Nazis spoke so well to their interests and inclinations."[9] Although Hitler never won a majority of German votes before coming to power, his level of popularity and support was very strong throughout the Third Reich.[10] Some Germans rose up against him, but always at great risk and as a tiny minority. The German children in this memoir who threw stones at young Margrit or who broke all the windows in the Rosenberg family home point toward another reality — those Germans willing to collaborate with the new German regime. And many more Germans would soon be perpetrating the crimes of the Holocaust itself.

The Norwegians and Swedes Margrit met acted quite differently from the Germans she had encountered. Norway accepted the Rosenberg family and gave them legal status when they fled Germany. Many individual Norwegians showed respect and compassion during the nearly three years the Rosenbergs lived in Norway. This included the many strangers who assisted them in their flight from Oslo into the safer, more remote countryside; the village policeman who never turned them in and warned them at moments of danger; and, especially, members of the Norwegian Underground, who offered them a dramatic and dangerous escape from Norway to Sweden when the German occupation threatened their survival. As Margrit notes in her memoir, she was later able to recommend one of those heroes, Einar Wellén, to Jerusalem's Holocaust Remembrance Center, Yad Vashem, which honoured him as one of the Righteous Among the Nations.

We see the best side of Norway in this memoir. There is more to that positive history, including a strong teachers' union that defied German efforts to enforce Nazi ideology in the schools. Lutheran clergy in Norway also showed courage in resisting Nazi efforts to control their message. However, there were other Norwegians who collaborated with the Nazi occupation. They formed their own version of the Nazi Party, the *Nasjonal Samling*, and Vidkun Quisling led a national Norwegian government that worked as a puppet under German control. Ultimately, Norway failed to protect the approximately 760 Jews who were sent to Auschwitz and murdered, more than one-third of the about seventeen-hundred Jews then living in Norway. Denmark, by comparison, dramatically rescued over ninety per cent of its Jewish population.[11]

The Danes are widely admired in Holocaust memory for their willingness and ability to save Jews. In October 1943, Danish citizens rose up to save more than seven thousand Jewish lives. Owners of fishing boats and even small rowboats ferried Jews across to the shores of Sweden. This is the best known and probably the most successful national effort of rescue during the Holocaust. The narrative of Denmark's resistance has some complications, however. For example, there is a myth that King Christian X of Denmark donned a yellow star himself and encouraged other Danes to wear a yellow star in order to protect Jews from being singled out. This did not happen. It is important to remember that the occupation of Denmark, based in part on the Nazi admiration for and desire to bond with Nordic peoples, was quite benign. Until 1943, Denmark was allowed to be largely self-governed, in part because Danes also agreed to cooperate with Germans. In actuality, the Danish effort to save Jews depended in part on German restraint. However, the act of saving more than seven thousand Jews remains remarkable.

Sweden, as well, played a largely positive role in the Holocaust, including as a place of refuge for Denmark's Jews. The country also provided refuge for many Norwegian Jews, including Margrit Rosenberg and her family. Margrit and her family felt relief as soon as they heard "Welcome to Sweden." The danger and the drama came to an end. However, this positive role played by Sweden was only possible because of Swedish neutrality during World War II, a stance that benefited the Swedish economy, made large quantities of iron ore available to the German machinery of war and left a generation of Norwegians somewhat angry at their Swedish neighbours.

Eventually, Margrit Rosenberg Stenge found refuge and a new life in Canada. A few years after the war had ended, Canada changed its policies to start generously welcoming Jewish refugees, at a time when the United States, for example, placed more restrictions on immigrants. Both nations had earlier made entry very difficult for Jews trying to escape the Holocaust. Residents of both Canada and the United States were hardly free of antisemitism in the first half of the twentieth century. It was only in the aftermath of the Holocaust that "respectable" antisemitism, now associated with Nazi Germany and the Holocaust, became widely discredited.

As we measure the nations Margrit experienced in her life, we can accurately contrast the violent antisemitism of the Germans at that time against the more welcoming actions and policies of the Norwegians, Swedes and Canadians. The Holocaust itself provides us the measuring stick. Today, nations and peoples who turn to violence and violate human rights are rightfully condemned. Nations and peoples who show compassion and respect human rights, by contrast, earn our admiration. By this measure, Margrit Rosenberg Stenge, through all the hardships she endured, was lucky to find her way to Norway, then to Sweden, and, finally, to Canada.

~

What will happen to Holocaust memory when all Holocaust survivors are gone? Margrit Rosenberg was only four years old when Adolf Hitler came to power, and that was nearly eighty-five years ago. We know that the living voice of survivor testimony will soon come to an end. Furthermore, there is a greying generation of Holocaust scholars who began their work in the 1970s and 1980s and are now entering retirement. Will they be replaced by a new generation of historians? Continued scholarship requires not only young scholars interested in this topic but also colleges and universities able to replace retiring faculty, which in times of tight finances is never a certainty.

There are several important responses to the question of Holocaust memory. First of all, as living voices disappear, this memoir and the other memoirs and filmed testimonies preserved by the Azrieli Foundation will maintain Holocaust memory. Other organizations do similar work, most notably the USC Shoah Foundation established by Steven Spielberg. The USC Shoah Foundation has created an archive of over fifty-five thousand video testimonies that preserve this history for future generations. Both Yad Vashem and the United States Holocaust Memorial Museum hold large archives that document the Holocaust and use extensive filmed testimony to teach visitors about past atrocities and the importance of preventing future genocides.

Perhaps the most important answer, however, involves the young. The story of the Holocaust can and should be passed to the next generation, and then from that generation to those who follow. One very important realization has developed in the past forty years: the lessons of the Holocaust are crucially important. The Holocaust is not just about Jewish victims. It is not just about German perpetrators (and their willing auxiliaries). It is a human story and a warning to all humans. It is the most graphic example in modern world history of how badly things go wrong when the most basic human values are distorted or lost. A better future requires that those who come after us focus on and continue to learn from the Holocaust.

Robert P. Ericksen
Kurt Mayer Chair in Holocaust Studies Emeritus
Pacific Lutheran University
Tacoma, Washington

March 2017

ENDNOTES

1 "Jewish Canadians," *The Canadian Encyclopedia*, www.thecanadianencyclopedia. ca. Other sources state that this number ranges between 30,000 to 40,000.

2 See, for example, Dorothy Rabinowitz, *New Lives: Survivors of the Holocaust Living in America* (New York: Avon Books, 1976). See also a short story by Philip Roth, "Eli, the Fanatic."

3 Thomas Blatt, *From the Ashes of Sobibor: A Story of Survival* (Evanston, IL: Northwestern University Press, 1997), xxi.

4 Richard Rashke, *Escape from Sobibor: The Heroic Story of the Jews who Escaped from a Nazi Death Camp* (New York: Houghton Mifflin, 1982).

5 See Deborah E. Lipstadt, *Beyond Belief: The American Press and the Coming of the Holocaust* (New York: Touchstone, 1993).

6 See Walter Laqueur, *The Terrible Secret: Suppression of the Truth about Hitler's "Final Solution"* (New York: Henry Holt, 1980).

7 The death toll of the Holocaust is commonly set at eleven million. This number includes six million Jews, the group most intensely targeted for annihilation. It also includes five million others, from Sinti and Roma to Russian prisoners of war, from members of the Polish intelligentsia to political opponents of the Nazi state, from the disabled murdered in a so-called program of euthanasia to gay men. In all cases, the eleven million were killed because of the Nazi ideology that considered them "life unworthy of life."

8 That condemnation includes the Genocide Convention, a policy established by the United Nations after World War II that bans genocide as an international crime against humanity.

9 Peter Fritzsche, *Germans into Nazis* (Cambridge, MA: Harvard University Press, 1998), 8.

10 See, for example, Robert P. Ericksen, *Complicity in the Holocaust: Churches and Universities in Nazi Germany* (New York: Cambridge University Press, 2012).

11 For an interesting description of Danish resistance, see Nathaniel Hong, *Occupied: Denmark's Adaptation and Resistance to German Occupation 1940–1945* (Copenhagen: Frihedsmuseet Venners Forlag, 2012).

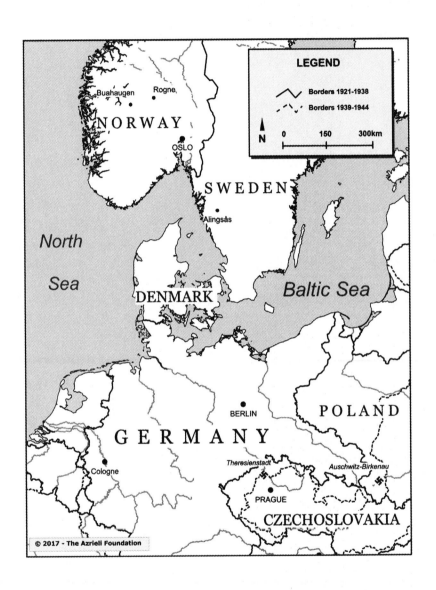

LEGEND

Borders 1921-1938
Borders 1939-1944

N

0   150   300km

Buahaugen   Rogne

NORWAY

OSLO

SWEDEN

Alingsås

North

Sea

DENMARK   Baltic Sea

POLAND

BERLIN

GERMANY

Cologne   Theresienstadt   Auschwitz-Birkenau

PRAGUE

CZECHOSLOVAKIA

© 2017 - The Azrieli Foundation

To my husband and best friend, Steven (Stefan) Stenge.

Acknowledgements

This book would not have been published without the generosity of the Azrieli Foundation. I would like to express my sincere appreciation to the Foundation and to Arielle Berger and Matt Carrington for their professional editing and to Mark Goldstein, the designer of the book cover, who captured the essence of my story.

My Early Years in Germany

My life began on December 27, 1928, in Cologne, Germany. I remember where we lived because, when I was a very young child, I was taught to say my home address just in case I got lost: "Akkrepiner Hof 4" (which I believe now to be Aggripinaufer). However, the chances of my getting lost were almost non-existent, since I always had a nanny watching over me.

I was very young when my parents and I lived in this apartment, so my memories of this first home are shadowy and vague. I believe there were many rooms in the apartment, all with high ceilings and large, tall windows through which I would stare on rainy days.

My parents, Alice and Max (Markus) Rosenberg, met during a family gathering. They were distantly related through marriage, and their attraction for each other was instant. When they got married, my mother was twenty-one years old and my father was thirty-three. The idea that opposites attract held true for my parents. My mother was a beautiful young woman, blond and blue-eyed, perhaps a bit heavier than is fashionable today. My father was slim, dark and handsome, shorter than my mother. Their temperaments were also very different. My mother's anger would flare up at the slightest provocation, although the storm would blow over quickly. My father, on the other hand, was calm and composed, but his rare outbursts of anger would be much more serious and longer lasting.

Even my parents' backgrounds were quite different. My mother
was an only child, and her childhood was a happy one. She grew up in
Germany in a small town called Beuel, near Bonn, where her father
was a merchant and made a comfortable living. In keeping with the
times, her mother stayed at home and looked after the household and
her only daughter. Like most German Jews, the family was German
first and Jewish second, and religion played a minor role in their lives.
My memories of my mother's parents, Simon and Selma Kaufmann,
are strictly visual: my grandfather was a short, heavy-set man, and
my grandmother was a grey-haired, stout lady. I saw them rarely and
did not know them well at all. I called them *Opa* (Grandpa) and *Oma*
(Grandma).

My father's family was much larger. I cannot say that I knew his
parents any better than my mother's, but I did see them more often.
They lived in the same house as some of my father's siblings, in a
town called Wächtersbach, near Frankfurt am Main. My grandfather
Jakob, who died when I was still very young, was wheelchair-bound
and had obviously had a stroke, but even today I can remember him
well. My grandmother Veilchen (Violet) suffered from severe asthma,
and, to relieve her symptoms, she would breathe in the fumes from
herbs that she would burn on a small plate. I can still picture her grey-
haired head bent over the plate. My father's brother Benjamin was
killed in World War I, where he fought for Germany against France.
My father's older sister, Selma, lived in a small town called Neuss with
her husband, Hermann Stein, and four children.

The care of my father's parents fell for the most part on *Tante*
(Aunt) Karolienchen, my father's sister, who lived with her husband,
Natan, in the family home. They had no children. Another brother,
Gustav, his wife, Selma, and their little girl, Elfriede, were also part
of the household. The men in the family were cattle traders, and my
father augmented their income when necessary.

My father's family in Wächtersbach was Orthodox, and my parents and I often spent the Jewish holidays with them, which gave

my cousin Elfriede and me a chance to get to know each other. As the years went by, we became quite close, since we were both only children.

When my parents announced to their families that they had decided to get married, I assume that the Wächtersbach family had some objections. Although my father was no longer religious, his family must have felt that marriage to a young woman from a completely liberal family would further estrange him from the beliefs of his youth. But the die was cast, and the two were wed. Their first-born child was a boy, who died in 1926 when he was only six weeks old.

I suppose that I must have been a rather lonely little girl in those early years in Germany. My companions were an assortment of young women, nannies or *Kindermädchen*, whom I would call *Fräulein* (Miss). My mother spent her days much like any other well-to-do young woman, shopping and playing bridge, while my father was at work in his paint manufacturing company, Kölner Farbenfabrik. My mother did not do any housework or cooking.

There was little interaction between me and my parents, whom I called *Mutti* (Mommy) and *Vati* (Daddy). I was allowed to say hello and curtsy to my mother's bridge friends. My mother would hug and kiss me in front of them, which embarrassed me. On Sundays, my father would also often play cards, a game called Skat, and he too would sometimes ask me to come and say hello. However, always sensitive to my needs, he would refrain from showing me his affection in his friends' company.

Another of my early and none too pleasant memories was the simple act of eating. In keeping with the times, I never ate with my parents but with the current Fräulein. Like many children, I had a small appetite, but since I had to eat everything that was on my plate, it would often take me hours to finish a meal. In the worst-case scenario, my mother would insist that I finish my leftover lunch at dinner, and only my father's intervention would rescue me.

When I was only four years old, my father became very ill. He had been a soldier in World War I and imprisoned by the French shortly after the war broke out. While in captivity, he gained proficiency in the French language, but the poor living conditions affected his health. His poor health became apparent when he suddenly became ill in 1932. The first diagnosis was diabetes, and, as if this were not enough, he was later found to be suffering from tuberculosis as well.

After that diagnosis, I saw my parents even less. They travelled frequently to Switzerland, where the air was said to be good for my father. Sometimes I would join them there with my nanny.

During the next few years, my father had several very serious operations, and my mother never left his side. When my father's health permitted it, my parents went on business trips, mainly to Scandinavia. Without my mother's constant and devoted care and attention, my father would undoubtedly have succumbed to his illnesses even more prematurely than he ultimately did.

My father's illness had a profound impact on me. From early childhood on and for years to come, I shared my mother's anxiety and worries. The rhythm of our family life always depended on my father's state of health. I was a very quiet little girl, always taking care not to disturb the gentle, loving man who was my Vati. A smile and a kiss from him made it all worthwhile — I loved him so.

There were also other serious changes on the horizon. Adolf Hitler came to power in 1933, and although this event had little immediate impact, if any, on our lives, it was not long until we began to feel the consequences of the political upheaval.

When I was six years old, I was enrolled in a neighbourhood school. An old photo in my mother's album shows me on my first day of school: a rather ordinary looking, smiling little girl with short brown hair, proudly displaying a colourful cone-shaped bag filled with candies. At the time, every student in Grade 1 was handed such a bag at the end of the first day of school.

Before school started the following year, I knew that something fundamental had changed in my life. I became aware that to be Jewish was to be different when I had to attend the Jewish school in Cologne rather than my old school nearby. This turned out to be a very good change. I loved my new teacher, who taught us not only reading, writing and arithmetic but also *Ivrit* (Hebrew), which opened a whole new world for me. My schoolmates came from all over the city. I formed many new friendships, but it was Vera who became my best friend. Our parents were friendly too, so Vera and I were able to see each other after school as well. Vera eventually immigrated to the United States with her parents, got married at an early age and unfortunately contracted polio shortly afterwards. She was in a wheelchair for the rest of her life and died many years ago.

Around 1934 or 1935, we moved into a new house at Marienburger Strasse 52 on a beautiful tree-lined street. There were a few living rooms, a large kitchen and several bedrooms upstairs. One of the downstairs rooms led out to a lovely garden with a fountain. Adjoining the service entrance was a dog kennel, which later housed a German shepherd dog.

In retrospect, I wonder at my parents' decision to buy this house at a time of considerable political unrest in Germany. However, this house at Marienburger Strasse 52 was my father's dream house. He and I often walked in the garden or sat on a bench there to have a quiet conversation — just the two of us. At that time, we had several servants, including a cook. The Fräulein, who occupied the room next to mine, was Jewish and the nicest nanny I ever had. She was also my last.

This house survived the war, which was a miracle. Cologne was bombed extensively by the Allies, but, as I learned years later, Marienburger Strasse 52 sustained only minor damage.

During the next few years, there were holiday trips to Italy with my parents and Fräulein, and my mother and father continued to travel without me on business. My father's health remained frail but manageable. One year a whooping cough epidemic broke out in Cologne, and because the doctor thought I had a mild case of the illness, I was immediately dispatched with my nanny to a region in Germany called the Schwarzwald, where the air was supposed to be good for my cough. I can still recall our walks through the woods and the wonderful scent of pine trees.

After changing schools, I came to realize that there was a certain stigma attached to being Jewish. I overheard conversations between my parents about Hitler and the antisemitism he preached, even though they did not yet believe that this had anything to do with them. As my father once told me, "Unsere Familie hat hier in Deutschland seit dem sechzehnten Jahrhundert gelebt" (Our family has lived here in Germany since the sixteenth century), so Hitler's policies could not possibly affect us. My father had even received the Iron Cross for bravery during World War I, and our home and business were in Germany. But as Hitler's voice was heard more frequently on the radio, my father grew exceedingly upset over Hitler's ranting and raving, which for the most part was directed against the Jews.

Our house and garden were set back from the street, and a low wall surrounded our property. One day, when I was in the garden playing by myself, a gang of young people gathered outside and started throwing rocks over the wall. When my father appeared, they ran off. My parents considered this incident extremely serious. Our home had been violated. That day in 1937 my childhood came to an end, and nothing was ever the same. I was never again allowed to leave our house unaccompanied, and my sense of security was gone forever.

I am absolutely certain that had we been able to leave Germany just then, we would have. But stringent laws had been passed prohibiting Jews from emigrating from Germany, and just as stringent were the laws and quota systems imposed in most countries, banning Jewish immigration. My father's medical history further complicated our situation.

My favourite Fräulein left, I believe, in 1937. I remember saying a tearful goodbye to her, feeling that my world was truly collapsing. But then — a big surprise. My cousin Erna, my father's sister's daughter, joined our household, and she became my all-time favourite companion. Erna, eleven years older than I, was a young woman with a sweet disposition who was always ready to pay attention to me. She was pretty, with fine features and beautiful curly hair. What I remember best is that she called me "Gritchen," which I loved.

Erna left for England with her older sister, Annie, in 1938. At the time, England admitted young Jewish women with the proviso that they work there as domestics, which both my cousins did until the end of the war. By then, they had earned their permanent residency in England. Annie remained in England all her life, married an Englishman, had a daughter, Sylvia, and eventually died in England. At the end of the war, Erna went back to Germany as an interpreter for the Allied forces, where she met her future husband, Erwin Brauner, also a German Jew. They settled in Birmingham, England. The rest of the family in Neuss, in response to the rise of the Nazis, spread around the world: my cousin Walter, the oldest in the family, made aliyah to Palestine and was one of the co-founders of Kibbutz HaZore'a, and my cousin Max, the youngest, immigrated to the United States. My father's sister Selma and her husband, Hermann, were deported and killed by the Germans.

~

In 1938, for reasons I have never understood, my parents decided to travel one more time on a short vacation in Italy with me. Letters had reached them from the family in Wächtersbach, indicating that antisemitic incidents had increased alarmingly. My father feared for our safety, and on our way back from Italy to Cologne, we stopped in Wächtersbach. That very night, shortly after my grandmother, Elfriede and I had gone to bed, we heard the now familiar sounds of broken glass.[1] I was terrified. An unruly mob had gathered out-

---

1 This event, occurring months earlier, foreshadows the infamous Night of Broken Glass, Kristallnacht. This series of pogroms took place in Germany and Austria

side our windows, most likely because they were aware of our presence. The stone bombardment continued for several hours. Almost every window in the house was shattered, and when a piece of glass was found in my grandmother's bed the following morning, it was obvious that the time for decisions had come.

Consequently, our whole family travelled back to Cologne by train the following morning. My uncles and aunts had packed only what was absolutely necessary. The decision for them to move to Cologne must have been extremely traumatic for everyone, except for Elfriede and me. I was so excited about the prospect of living in the same house as my cousin that nothing else mattered at the time, and for Elfriede, too, this seemed a wonderful new adventure.

The reason for this move was that the bigger cities were considered safer than the villages and towns. There were fewer Jews living in the smaller places, which made them more vulnerable, and my parents felt that the family would be safer in Cologne than in the small town that had been their home.

The next few months were difficult for all the adults in our house. My mother was not used to life with a big family, and all the maids had left because, according to Hitler's new laws, they could no longer be employed by Jews. My aunts were used to doing their own housework and took care of everything, and I remember well how we all ate together around a large table in the dining room. This was a welcome change for me, since I was used to having my meals with only my Fräulein, and for the first time in my life no one paid any attention to how much or how little I ate. Elfriede and I attended school as if everything were normal, and this time we spent together in Cologne so long ago has kept us close throughout our lives.

---

between November 9 and 10, 1938. Over the course of twenty-four hours, ninety-one Jews were murdered, 25,000 to 30,000 were arrested and deported to concentration camps, two hundred synagogues were destroyed and thousands of Jewish businesses and homes were ransacked.

In 1938, the situation became more precarious each day. *Onkel* (Uncle) Gustav had applied for an immigration visa to the United States earlier on and expected to hear from the American consulate any day. Tante Selma's brother, who lived in Bridgeport, Connecticut, had acted as guarantor for his sister and her family. Without such a guarantor, it was virtually impossible at that time to obtain a visa to the States.

By September 1938, my parents had become very nervous. My father was not strong enough physically to deal effectively with the major problems facing us all, and it was my mother's decision that she and Vati go on one more business trip, albeit this time with a different purpose — to look for a country in which we could find refuge. It was still possible to leave Germany for short periods of time. My parents decided to bring along the chemical formulas for my father's own particular brand of house paint, in order to exchange them for possible employment. I can still picture the slim volumes in black bindings that contained probably his most valuable assets at the time. Smuggling the formulas out of the country was dangerous, but my parents felt they had no choice.

Since Cologne was then in the grip of a polio epidemic, the schools were closed. At dinner the evening before my parents were supposed to leave, I suddenly burst into tears and told them that this time I did not want to be left behind, ostensibly because of the polio epidemic. In truth, there were other reasons why I could not bear to be separated from my parents then. I did not really know my aunts and uncles well; they were a tight-knit family and I felt like an outsider. The entire situation in our household was very unusual and strange. Being a rather perceptive and grown-up little girl, I knew that life in Germany was becoming more dangerous each day, and I worried that I might never see my parents again.

This was unusual behaviour for the docile little girl who had been left behind on many occasions with only a nanny as company. I suppose my display of emotion at the time impressed upon my parents that it would not be wise to leave me behind, even though our destination was still unknown. Since my father had business connections in Brussels, this would be our first stop.

The following morning we boarded a train with the hope that Belgium would be the country where we would be able to find our new home. Little did I know that I would not return to Cologne and that I would never again see my grandmother, Tante Karolienchen and Onkel Natan.

My grandmother died in Cologne in 1940 and is buried there.

After being sent to live in a Jewish house in Cologne, Tante Karolienchen and Onkel Natan were deported to Riga, from where they never returned.

I didn't know my mother's parents' fate until my son visited the United States Holocaust Memorial Museum in Washington decades after the war and looked for their names on a computer register. He found both my grandparents' names, with a note saying that they had been deported first to Theresienstadt and then to Auschwitz, where they perished.

My First Cruise

Despite the fact that I left the country of my birth more than a lifetime ago, in my heart I know that the little German Jewish girl I was still lives deep inside me. My life's journey has taken me to several countries, but if truth be told, I do not feel that any of them is my own. Germany is only the country where I happened to be born, but when I hear certain *Lieder* (songs) or German expressions that remind me of my childhood, I feel an unexplainable sadness. At times I have been called a *Jecke*, a less than flattering expression for a German Jew, because of certain traits I have always had, such as being hardworking and organized. True, these are German characteristics, but in my case they are my father's legacy.

After arriving in Belgium, it soon became apparent that there were no business opportunities for my father there, and my parents decided to continue on to Scandinavia, where he was well known. But there was a major problem. Taking me along on a journey like this was out of the question. My father needed all of my mother's attention and care, and I would simply be an additional burden.

My parents had met the Nussbaum family while they were still living in Germany. The Nussbaums had been able to leave Germany and had settled in Brussels. A quick solution to our travel problem had to be found, and my parents got in touch with *Herr* (Mr.) and *Frau* (Mrs.) Nussbaum to inquire if they could possibly look after me until such time that our situation resolved itself. They agreed. In retrospect, I assume that the Nussbaums were well paid for their efforts. After all, they, too, were refugees, and the extra income would have been welcome. This was the first time that my parents had to make an unusual decision that concerned me — to leave me in the hands of virtual strangers. It would by no means be the last time that I was put to the test.

Instead of being with family in Cologne, I was now with strangers in Brussels, but I quickly adjusted to my new life and soon came to love it. The Nussbaums were an extraordinary family and quite different from mine. They had three children — a boy older than I, a younger girl and a small baby whose gender I do not remember. Frau Nussbaum was in the early stages of another pregnancy, which none of the children including myself was aware of. They were a warm, close-knit Orthodox Jewish family, where Shabbat and Jewish holidays were strictly observed, and I loved being a part of their lives.

The Nussbaums' apartment was beautifully furnished. Persian carpets covered the floors of the living and dining rooms. A piano stood in the corner of the living room. The Nussbaums had likely left Germany before restrictions were imposed, so that they had been able to take some of their belongings with them.

I did not go to school during the three months I stayed in Brussels, but I did manage to learn some French and spent my days with Frau Nussbaum and the younger children. Frau Nussbaum was a wonderfully patient mother, who obviously enjoyed spending time with us children. She would read to us, play simple little melodies on the piano and take us for walks while Herr Nussbaum was at work. I did not want to think of the day that I would have to leave my new family.

In the meantime, my parents had visited Sweden and Denmark without any luck. But all that changed when they came to Oslo, Norway. My father contacted Nordiske Destillationsverker, a fairly large company and a customer of Kölner Farbenfabrik, and offered them his paint formulas in exchange for a position. The people at Nordiske obviously recognized the value of such a proposal and promised my father the position of director of their new paint manufacturing division. Proof of employment guaranteed a work permit for my father and Norwegian immigration visas for both my parents.

With these documents in hand, my parents returned briefly to Germany to try to salvage some household goods with which to begin our lives in Norway. Our family was still living in our house on Marienburger Strasse, and it must have been unimaginably painful for my parents to say goodbye to them, not knowing what the future held in store for any of us.

As soon as they were able to, my parents rented a tiny furnished apartment at Kirkeveien 104 in Oslo, consisting of a living room with a bed that folded into the wall (a Murphy bed), a bedroom, a kitchen and a bath. Vati started his new career and so did my mother — housekeeping. This change was very difficult for her, since in all her thirty-six years she had never done any of the housework. Being in a foreign country made things even more difficult for her. True, she had been to Norway many times before, but always as a guest in hotels or in people's homes, and even the language, although it was familiar, was strange once she had to use it on a daily basis. My father adapted quickly to his new surroundings. His colleagues were supportive, and it did not take long for the new paint division to prosper under my father's leadership.

But I was still in Belgium. Although my father applied for my immigration visa as quickly as he was able to, it took much longer than expected to receive this document. It was unheard of to keep a child separated from her parents for any length of time for lack of a visa, but it was rumoured that one of the Norwegian immigration officials was a Nazi, and he caused one delay after another. Finally, in late December 1938, the visa arrived.

As soon as I received my ticket for the crossing to Oslo, Herr Nussbaum began looking for someone who was scheduled to sail to

Norway on the same ship as I was and who would be willing to keep an eye on me during the trip. Herr Stern, a middle-aged German Jewish businessman, fit the bill — that is, at least he was booked on the same ship as I was. That he seemed to have little or no experience with young children was another matter.

It was a sad little girl who parted from the Nussbaums in early January 1939. They left me at the pier in the care of Herr Stern, and the two of us boarded the ship that would take us to Norway. I remember very little of our voyage, except that I was lonely and frightened. Herr Stern's cabin was on a different deck than mine, so he checked on me once or twice a day, and, for the rest of the day, I mostly stayed in my cabin reading. On the second day of our trip, I ventured on deck to look for Herr Stern in his cabin. The wind was blowing, and I struggled with the door leading to a different part of the ship. I could not open it, but another passenger came to my rescue and then addressed me in a language I did not know. Fortunately, I did not get seasick during the voyage. On the third day, we arrived in Oslo.

It was a cold, dark winter day, such as you find in the North in the middle of winter. I was nervous and apprehensive. Not only was I arriving in a new country, but I knew that my life with my parents would be very different than it had been until now. My parents had told me that we were poor now, so I was wondering what that meant. It would be the very first time the three of us lived by ourselves, without servants or relatives. Would Mutti still be impatient with me? What would school be like in Norway? A million thoughts whirred through my head while I looked for my parents as the ship approached the wharf.

Finally I saw them, bundled up in their winter clothes, eagerly looking for me. A great feeling of relief surged through me. I thought everything would be all right.

Norway on the Cusp

At first my life in Norway was totally confusing. Everything was different from what I had been accustomed to. I slept on the Murphy bed in the living room, instead of in my own room. My mother did the food shopping, cooking and cleaning. Walking through the streets of Oslo, I heard a language I did not understand.

It was imperative that I start school as soon as possible, since I had missed more than four months already. So a few days after I arrived in Oslo, my mother took me to a neighbourhood school and tried as best she could to explain the situation to the principal. The principal suggested that I start Grade 4, which in fact was the appropriate grade for my age (ten). I would just listen in the beginning and do as much homework as I could. The principal assured my mother that I would learn the language in no time at all because I was still very young. Little did he know just how quickly I would speak and act like any other Norwegian little girl! My mother also enrolled me in cheder, Jewish classes attended after regular school. I met Jewish children my age there, and one of them, Celia Century, became my lifelong friend.

My first day of school was quite an event. All the girls in the class wanted to be my friend; I was a celebrity, a girl who could not speak their language. But it was Else who became my best friend. Every afternoon, she came to our apartment and we did our homework together. Since there was no other way to communicate, I had to try to speak to her in Norwegian. With Else's encouragement, it took only about three months until I was able to speak Norwegian fluently, without a trace of a German accent. It was not long before I refused to speak German to my parents in public, such as on streetcars or in stores. I was doing well in school and was soon a better student than my mentor Else.

On their many business trips to Norway, my parents had befriended the Meiranovsky family. Now that we were settled, the Meiranovskys, despite their age difference, became my parents' closest friends. Moritz and Rosa Meiranovsky had five adult sons. One son, Elias, lived in the United States, and four sons — two of whom were married — lived in Oslo. The youngest, Sigmund, who was nineteen years old, was my hero. To Sigmund, I was the little sister he never had, and he was very proud of me, mainly because of my scholastic achievements. He taught me to ski and took me on hikes in the mountainous areas around Oslo. I also became very close to his brother John, who had recently married Beks. John and Beks lived in a lovely new apartment, and I was always welcome in their home.

The Meiranovskys also introduced me to a language that was entirely new to me — Yiddish, which was spoken mostly by East European Jews. The majority of the Jews in Norway (only about seventeen hundred souls) had originally come from East European countries, and the older generation still spoke Yiddish at home. Yiddish is a colourful, expressive and melodious language, which was rarely, if ever, heard in Germany at the time.

The descendants of Rosa and Moritz Meiranovsky (later changed to Meieran) played a very important role in my life. Sigmund left Oslo on April 11, 1940, to join the Norwegian army in an unoccupied area. It was not long, however, before Norway had to surrender completely to the Germans. Sigmund escaped to Sweden and made his way from there to the United States. He decided to get back into the fight against the Germans and went to Toronto, where he joined a contingent of Norwegians who were training to become airmen at a place called Little Norway. Upon completion of their training, the airmen went to England, from where they flew bombing missions over Germany. Sigmund was shot down and taken prisoner of war. He managed to hide the fact that he was Jewish and tried to escape numerous times, unfortunately with little success. After liberation, he returned to Norway for a short while and then immigrated to the United States.

During World War II, John and Beks fled to Sweden. They returned to Oslo in 1945. After the war, Beks and John were my family's closest friends. When I got married, this friendship extended to my husband.

The summer of 1939, my first summer in Norway, was a calm and quite carefree time — at least for me. My parents and I moved into a larger apartment in an adjoining building on Kirkeveien road, in which I had my own bedroom. Although she occasionally lost her patience, my mother seemed to adjust quite well. My father's health was better than it had been for a long time, despite the fact that he had a festering wound on his back, which refused to heal because of his diabetes. No one knew about this problem except the family doctor, my mother and me. The wound needed a new dressing every day, which my mother tirelessly took care of.

The days were long and bright, and for a ten-year-old girl there was always something to do. I played hopscotch with my friends on the sidewalk outside our building and often went to see our new neighbour, *Fru* (Mrs.) Prager, when she was at home. Herr and Fru Prager, in their late fifties, were Jewish and childless and seemed to enjoy my visits. During the day, Fru Prager often helped out in her mother's candy store. Our friends Beks and John lived very close by, and I would walk over to their apartment in the late afternoon to say hello. On Sundays, we would sometimes take the ferry to Bygdø, a peninsula in the Oslo Fjord, to go swimming. That was always the highlight of the week.

In the fall of 1939, I began Grade 5 and felt quite grown up. Norwegian newspapers and radio broadcasts were full of news about the war in Europe. But it was far away and did not concern me — or so I thought. My parents were in constant touch by letters with our family in Cologne. They were still living in the house on Marienburger Strasse. Onkel Gustav was still waiting for his visa. Realizing the danger that our family was in, my mother urged my aunt and uncle to let Elfriede come to Norway while they waited for their visa. This was an extremely difficult decision for Onkel Gustav and Tante Selma. It was one thing to part from your only child for a few months, knowing that you would see each other again, but quite another to send your daughter off all by herself, while you were unable to leave and did not know what lay ahead.

Late in 1939, Elfriede also arrived in Oslo by ship, without her family, as I had before her. The following months were not easy for her. Although happy to be with me, she was often homesick for her parents. She did not start school because my parents hoped that my aunt and uncle would receive their visa soon and come to Norway to pick up Elfriede on their way to the United States. It would be more than three months until they arrived.

By the beginning of April 1940, the threat of war was palpable even in Norway. Almost by a miracle, Tante Selma and Onkel Gustav received their visa and came to Oslo. We were happy to finally be together again, but we knew it could not last. By then, both Elfriede and I were eleven years old and understood that a long separation might be ahead of us. The day of departure came all too soon. My uncle and my father were inconsolable the evening before the departure. They had always been very close, and they feared that they would never meet again.

On April 4, we accompanied my aunt and uncle and Elfriede to a ship. They went on board only to be told that they would have to disembark and take a train to Bergen, where the ship would meet them.

No explanation was given. What could this mean? That evening, we were all upset and apprehensive, and after a sleepless night we once again said our goodbyes, this time at the train station. Despite the delay, they managed to get away in time.

Four days later, the war broke out in Norway.

Tracks in the Snow

By April 8, 1940, my father knew that a German attack on Norway was imminent. Before going to work that morning, he asked my mother to go to our bank and withdraw a considerable amount of money in order to be prepared for any eventuality. However, my mother decided to postpone the banking until the following day because she had other plans, a decision that would prove to have very serious consequences.

Norway was ill-prepared for an attack. There were no bomb shelters to speak of, and the air raid sirens that woke us in the middle of the following night caught the population of Oslo by surprise. Although my father knew that the makeshift bomb shelter in the basement of our building would not protect us from a direct hit, he nevertheless insisted that we join the other residents there. It was dark and crowded in the relatively small room, and everyone was nervous and frightened. Our peace had been short-lived. What would become of us? Where could we go?

My father knew with absolute certainty that we had to get away. During the past year, he had on two occasions visited the German consulate. I am not sure why, but I know that he had lost his temper both times he had been there. No doubt our name was blacklisted at the consulate, and we could be easily located. As former German citizens, albeit declared "stateless" (citizens of no country) by that time, we were even more vulnerable.

In the cellar during the air raid, my father formulated a vague plan: he would ask someone at Nordiske, his workplace, to drive us out of the city. We went upstairs as soon as the all-clear signal sounded, and my father made his phone call and actually convinced one of the salespeople at the company to agree to his plan. We immediately started to pack, ensuring we took an adequate supply of insulin and syringes for my father, who injected himself with insulin two or three times a day. We packed only a few pieces of clothing for each of us, since we had no idea of how we would travel, for how long or where we would end up.

While waiting for my father's colleague, my parents realized that, in addition to all our other problems, we had insufficient funds. Despite the early hour, my mother rang the doorbell of Herr and Fru Prager. They lent us a few hundred *kroner*, the Norwegian currency, which was not a large sum of money and did little to alleviate my parents' concerns.

It was still early morning when my father's colleague arrived in his small car. War was in the air, and many people had already taken to the roads leading to the countryside, where they felt it would be safer. In Oslo, there had been no snow, but when we got farther away from the city, it became apparent that winter had not lost its grip. The lakes were still frozen, and there were icy patches on the road. After a couple of hours' drive, the car stopped at an inn. My father's co-worker told us that he had to return to Oslo to look after his own family. He had done us an enormous favour under difficult circumstances, and we were forever grateful to him.

We spent the rest of the day at the country inn, which gradually filled to capacity. Everyone spoke to everyone else about the war. My parents soon realized that the other people in the day room had noticed us and were beginning to wonder about us. Not only were we foreigners, but my parents' accent betrayed our origin. In a country that was under attack by the Germans, this was a most undesirable position to be in. So my father decided that he had better tell the truth about us, who and what we were and that we were in urgent need of a safe place to stay.

Since there were only about seventeen hundred Jewish people in Norway at the time, many Norwegians we encountered then and later during the war had never even met a Jew. Nevertheless, in the tense atmosphere of the little inn, people seemed to understand our plight, and a man came forward and told us that he knew of an electrician in a remote village who might be willing to take us in to augment his income. The name of the village was Rogne, located in the Valdres region.

Although we had never heard of this area, we then had a destination, a goal. The following day, we were able to get rides on a truck, a milk wagon and a horse and carriage, arriving late in the day in Rogne. Since the electrician, Nils Granli, and his wife, Alma, were well known in the village, we were directed to their house. A steep dirt road led up to a comfortable-looking, green painted house above the highway.

Alma had obviously seen our approach through the window and opened the door before we even had a chance to knock. When we told her that we had been sent by one of Nils's customers, she immediately let us in.

At the time, Nils was approximately forty-five years old. Alma was a few years his junior, and they had a little girl, then about a year and a half. We never found out how this lovely, cultured woman ended up in such a remote place as Rogne and married to Nils. She had been a governess in France when she was younger, and she was surprised and delighted when she heard that my father also spoke French. The common language immediately forged a bond between the two of them.

We explained to Nils and Alma that we were Jews originally from Germany, yet they both readily agreed to rent us a room in their house with kitchen privileges. I don't think that they quite realized how our presence in their home put them in grave danger. Nils did understand, however, that our situation warranted the protection of the *lensmann* (police officer) in the village, whom he considered completely trustworthy. He went to see him immediately and returned with the assurance that the *lensmann* would not give us away and would do everything in his power to protect us. We had no choice but to trust him.

Alma's life was a difficult one. As we discovered somewhat later, Nils was an alcoholic, with the unpredictable temper and behaviour of an addict. We stayed away from him when he drank, but Alma had no such option. For this reason, I believe that our presence in their home might have been somewhat of a comfort to Alma and a distraction from her worries. Nils and Alma were not farmers, but they kept a cow and a pig in the barn adjacent to their house. The cow supplied our milk, and each Christmas Nils and Alma slaughtered a pig. There was never any shortage of food in their household.

That first night, we gathered around the radio and listened to the news. The war was raging on several fronts, but it seemed to us that the situation was desperate and that it would not be long until Norway, too, would be under Hitler's rule.

The following day brought the war close to Rogne. Around noon, the air raid siren sounded in the village, and all of us in the house, as well as the neighbours, ran into the dense forest nearby. Suddenly, an airplane appeared overhead, and before we realized fully what was happening, the sound of gunfire tore through the air. I looked up for a minute and saw to my horror the face of the German pilot as he flew low to the ground. And just as suddenly, I was lying on the ground with my father's body protecting me, while he ordered everyone else to lie down wherever they were. By some miracle, only one person was injured. That day my father became my hero forever, and he gained the respect of all the people who were with us in the forest.

Later that day, my parents went for a walk along the highway. A German plane flew overhead, and when the pilot saw them, he began shooting. Only my father's presence of mind saved their lives: they both jumped into the ditch next to the highway and escaped injury.

That night, some friends and neighbours of the Granlis suggested that we all move to an area higher up in the mountains. Equipped with knapsacks filled with provisions, we set out during the night, walking for miles through the deep snow. Besides all our other concerns, my mother and I worried about whether my father would be able to keep up the pace. But as usual, Vati did not complain, and eventually we all reached our destination, a small cabin, where we spent the rest of the night and part of the next day. Then word reached us that the fighting in Norway was over and that the Norwegians had capitulated to the Germans. We all returned to Rogne.

Now that the fighting was officially over, I was allowed to play with the other children on the road below the Granlis' house. This road was also the main highway in the area. I did not understand the dialect of the region, known as New Norwegian, but the games children play everywhere are similar, and after the tension of the last week, it felt wonderful to run around with my new playmates. Schools were still closed because of the war, although the German occupation was now a *fait accompli*.

A few days later, on a balmy spring day with the sun melting the snow on the road, I was again playing with my friends. Suddenly, a jeep with four German officers approached. Imagine my horror when they stopped and asked me in German for directions to the police officer in the village. German was my mother tongue, which I spoke with my parents every day. But now it was spoken by the enemy, and I knew that if I answered in German, the officers would immediately become suspicious. How could a little girl in a mountain village speak German so well? With my heart almost jumping out of my chest, I pretended not to understand, and they drove off. Although I was just an eleven-year-old girl, I think those few minutes ended what was left of my childhood.

Although the village school re-opened shortly after this incident, my parents worried that it would be too risky for us if they allowed me to attend. So for me, Grade 5 lasted from August 1939 until April 8,

1940. I missed going to school with the other children. At that point, all I wanted was to be like everyone else. But of course I was different.

A few days after the incident with the German officers, the *lensmann* paid us a visit. He reiterated what Nils had already told us, that we would be quite safe in Rogne and that we would have nothing to fear from the villagers in the area. He did not know any Nazis or anyone who had ever met a Jewish person. He assured us he had no intention of becoming a Nazi collaborator and that he would give us ample warning should the situation warrant it. We agreed with Nils that the *lensmann* could be trusted.

Unfortunately for the *lensmann*, he joined the Nazi Party a few years later. His reasoning was that if he did not join the party, the occupation forces would remove him and appoint a real Nazi to fill his position, which would be much worse for the villagers. What he didn't realize was that, in his new role, he would have to arrest people, even his own friends, who were known to be anti-Nazi, most of whom were teachers. These arrests caused him to be treated like a war criminal after the war, and he was ultimately brought to trial. My parents were called as witnesses for the defence, and he was not imprisoned. However, his reputation was irreparably damaged and his life ruined.

My family's most serious immediate problem was a lack of money. We needed funds to pay Nils and Alma rent and to buy groceries. Since no one could foresee how long the German occupation of Norway would last, my parents were faced with a difficult decision. One of us had to return to Oslo to withdraw our family's savings. My father was completely ruled out because his dark hair and prominent nose — stereotypical Jewish traits — would make him much too conspicuous. With her blond hair and blue eyes, my mother did not look like a foreigner, but she and my father both spoke Norwegian with a German accent. A Norwegian police officer might consider her the enemy and treat her accordingly. An encounter with a German would also have disastrous results for my mother. That left only me. I have often wondered how my parents could send their only child on such a mission. It must have been out of desperation, because they both would have known that I might not succeed in the mission or, even worse, might never return.

My parents found a truck driver who had to drive to Oslo and back the following day. Equipped with a signed power-of-attorney document for our Oslo neighbour Fru Prager and the telephone number of my father's former employer, Nordiske Destillationsverker, I climbed into the cab with the driver. We travelled in complete silence, mainly I suppose because the driver did not quite know what to say to me. I assume he was just as worried as I was about being stopped on the road. What was he doing with a little girl without any kind of identification? When he let me off on Kirkeveien road, I was greatly relieved.

My parents had advised Fru Prager that I was coming to Oslo, so she was waiting for me in her apartment. We headed for the neighbourhood bank immediately. I was nervous and fearful when we entered the bank, and I was sure everyone could hear the loud pounding of my heart. I need not have worried. Fru Prager gave the bank clerk the power-of-attorney document, and we withdrew my family's savings without any difficulties.

Later that day, Fru Prager told me that my father's intuition had been right — a few days after the takeover, two Germans in civilian clothes had come to our apartment to look for us. When they found no one there, they asked some of the neighbours if they knew where we were, and they truthfully replied that they did not. The Pragers had not been at home at the time.

Fru Prager phoned Nordiske to advise them of my family's whereabouts. My father's colleagues were relieved when they heard that we were safe. Throughout the next almost three years that we spent in hiding in Rogne, my father's co-workers took turns coming to see us, always bringing enough money to last us until the next visit. Although we needed this money desperately, my father always felt embarrassed when the envelope was handed to him. How would he ever repay Nordiske? His colleagues insisted, however, that these payments were merely royalties derived from his formulas — and his due. The generosity of Nordiske Destillationsverker was instrumental in saving our lives.

In May 1940, the *lensmann* came to see us again, this time with the news that he had received directives from the occupation forces that every person in his area had to be registered and issued identification papers. Since this posed a certain danger to us, he suggested that we move to the mountain range above Rogne for the summer. It would be safer there, and by the time we returned in the fall, no one would be looking for people to register — at least that is what he hoped.

The Norwegian farmers move with their cattle to the mountains above their villages during the summer. Here their cows and goats graze freely on the lush mountain grass in the higher elevations. These little mountain villages are called *seter* and consist mainly of small primitive cabins without electricity or other amenities.

We had heard of a nice log cabin in a *seter* called Buahaugen that was for rent, and one fine day in June, Nils drove us there in his truck. Like all the other cabins, ours was without running water or electricity, and there was an outhouse behind the cabin. Buahaugen lay above the treeline, so mainly low bushes grew there with just an occasional small birch tree. The cabin overlooked two lakes, the Vansjø and the Royri, which were joined by a brook and surrounded by mountains.

In the beginning, we were almost alone up there, but toward the middle of June, farmers began moving up, and we were glad to have people around. Living in the *seter* was not easy, and our whole lifestyle changed dramatically. We had to fetch water from the brook — fresh and cold water — which my mother and I did. My father cut the wood for heating and cooking. No one in Germany would have believed that he would be able to do such hard physical work ever again. He felt really well in the fresh mountain air, although the sore on his back never healed. Fortunately, we were able to get his insulin from an apothecary in Fagernes, a small town not far from Rogne, who sent the preparation to Nils at regular intervals.

We were very fortunate to be able to spend the summer months at Buahaugen. It was a quiet, tranquil life. Each morning, we were awoken by the tinkle of cowbells as the cows were led out to pasture. A young girl, Martha, who became one of my best friends in the *seter*, delivered fresh milk every morning. I played on the rocks at the water's edge with all the other children, and sometimes in really hot weather we went swimming in the ice-cold lakes. We watched the women make goat cheese in huge black kettles, and when they were finished, we scraped the kettles clean. This cheese was a delicacy. On midsummer nights, we feasted on *rømmegrøt*, a type of Norwegian porridge made from sour cream. I cannot possibly describe its wonderful taste. We often climbed the mountain above Buahaugen to pick blueberries and cloudberries, yellow berries that resemble raspberries but with a completely different taste. The women made jam with these berries, and the cloudberries were also mixed with whipped cream for Sunday dessert.

My parents learned to fish for trout and other kinds of fish in the lake. They usually fished from a rowboat, but on balmy summer evenings, the three of us took our fishing rods to the large stones protruding into the lakes and fished for smaller fish from there. With help from a neighbour, my father built a makeshift oven of rocks outside our cabin, in which he smoked some of the trout he caught, and my mother stored some of this fish for the winter months ahead. We were never short on food.

In the fall of 1940, we had no other choice but to move back to Nils and Alma's house in Rogne. Despite the inconveniences of living in a primitive log cabin in Buahaugen, we had been more comfortable there. I had my own bedroom, and we had a spacious living room and kitchen. At the Granlis' house, we shared one room. It was, however, impossible to stay in the *seter* in the winter because of all the snow, the difficulty in getting provisions and the utter isolation.

When I returned to Buahaugen in 1994, much had changed. I could still see the remnants of the primitive oven we had used in the underbrush near the steps of our burnt-down cottage. During a raid in the summer of 1943, the Germans set fire to all the cabins in Buahaugen. Forests of birch trees surrounded the many new cottages that had been built and that belonged mostly to city dwellers. Only a few farmers brought their cattle up to Buahaugen by that time, since other *seters* were more convenient. Many of the cabins and cottages still had no electricity, but complicated installations provided running water to most of the summer homes and electricity had been promised. Buahaugen has become a popular summer and spring ski resort of sorts and is easily accessible from the highway that goes to Rogne, only about twenty minutes by car. In the winter, the gravel road from Rogne is closed.

In September, my parents decided that I could not afford to miss any more schooling, so I began Grade 6 in a one-room schoolhouse in the next village, Volbu. Volbu was across the lake that was visible from the Granlis' house and could be reached by walking or cycling around the lake in the spring, summer and fall or by crossing the frozen lake on skis or with a *spark* in the winter. A *spark*, known as a "kicksled" in English, is like a chair mounted on runners. Its rider stands behind it and kicks the ground to propel it forward. These sleds were a very useful mode of transportation on icy or snow-packed surfaces, and in those days they were also extensively used as baby carriages in the winter.

To my surprise, children attended school only every other day. By this time, I understood the dialect of the region perfectly, but I had to learn to write it as well. I loved school because it lent some sense of normalcy to my life.

News travels fast in the countryside, and when I started school, many of the villagers knew that we were Jewish, although they really did not know what that meant. I believe that none of them had ever met a Jew before. We heard that there were now a few Nazi sympathizers in the village, but it was thought that they would not pose any danger, and in fact they did not. Gudrun, a very intelligent girl in my grade, was the daughter of such a sympathizer. When she invited me to her house for dinner one day, my parents debated whether I should go. Was there a sinister motive behind the invitation? In the end, my parents thought that it might do more harm than good not to accept the invitation. Perhaps Gudrun's parents, having never met a Jewish person before, were curious about the Jewish girl who had become their daughter's schoolmate. I was somewhat uneasy in their company, although they were very pleasant and did not even ask any unusual questions.

On my trip to Buahaugen in 1994, I met a man who remembered that he had gone to school with me, although he was a few years younger than I. I asked him if he knew anything about Gudrun, and he told me that she was now living in Lillehammer, Norway, with her family and that she had become a teacher.

My parents' lives were difficult. They were totally isolated, with Nils and Alma as their only company. My father was often very depressed. Even though he should have had regular medical checkups, he did not dare go to a doctor. We also did not have dental care during those years, and my mother had to pry the braces off my teeth when the war broke out. To pass the time, my parents went for walks in good weather, my mother knitted endlessly and they both read voraciously anything they could get hold of.

Although my life was far from normal, I still had some kind of routine. I did my homework, which there was a lot of, my mother taught me how to knit and I, too, read a great deal. Alma taught me how to milk the cow, so I would from time to time relieve her of this work. I actually liked to help Alma with her chores because she was always pleasant company. But nothing was more fun than the Christmas preparations. The house filled up with the delicious fragrance of freshly baked cookies mixed with burning wood from the stove. Alma cleaned house from morning to night, until everything sparkled. In the living room, the lights of the Christmas tree blinked on and off, and the house looked peaceful and pleasant. How I wished that I could be a part of all the celebration surrounding Christmas! But I could not. I turned twelve years old that winter and was, in the Jewish tradition, considered a woman. As a Jewish woman, I was quite aware that I had different obligations.

That winter I participated in skiing competitions, both downhill and slalom. I was never much good at either because I was scared of falling. As a matter of fact, when I came down the hills, some of my friends would exclaim, "Here comes the *lensmann*," because our chief of police was known to be slow. It upset me that I was not better at this popular sport, because I was always ambitious. But no matter how hard I tried, I never won a skiing competition. Cross-country skiing was a way of life in the village so was not considered a sport.

While the war was raging in Europe, we lived in relative tranquility in our secluded village. My parents, however, were never at ease. Coupled with their concerns about our own future were the worries about the family they had left behind in Germany. Finding out that Tante Selma, Onkel Gustav and Elfriede had arrived safely in the United States was a great relief.

The Germans were stationed in Fagernes and communicated with the *lensmann* only from time to time. We were no longer permitted to own radios, but we broke this rule, and on dark winter nights we would sit around the radio trying to tune in to the BBC, the British Broadcasting Corporation. Sometimes we would hear Hitler speak, which totally infuriated my father and depressed him for hours on end. The war was not going well for the Allied forces.

We were happy to return to Buahaugen in the summer of 1941. It had been a long and difficult winter with the Granlis. Nils had gone on drinking binges, and we had worried that he would one day spill our secrets when under the influence of alcohol. Our log cabin was waiting for us, and now that we knew what to expect, the summer seemed like a welcome reprieve.

That summer we had a visitor. Mr. Meiranovsky arrived from Oslo to spend a week with us. What a welcome surprise! My parents' pleasure at being with their long-time friend was palpable. But the visit was also a time for reflection. In my mind's eye, I can see my father and Mr. Meiranovsky sitting on a large stone overlooking the Vansjø, the large lake, while my father warned his friend of the danger that he and the entire Norwegian Jewish population would face if they remained in Norway. I happened to overhear this conversation: my father advised Mr. Meiranovsky to persuade his whole family to try to escape to Sweden. Sweden was a neutral country, and many Norwegians had already crossed the border to escape the German occupation. However, like so many others, Mr. Meiranovsky did not believe that any harm would come to the Jews in Oslo. They were Norwegians, and the Germans would not dare to persecute them, he thought. How wrong he was! That was the last time we saw Moritz Meiranovsky. The elder Meiranovskys were ultimately deported to Auschwitz with two of their sons and their families. All perished in the camp.

A neighbouring cottage in Buahaugen was owned by an attorney, Mr. Wellén, whose nephew Einar came to visit each summer. My father often spoke to the elder Wellén, and that summer of 1941 he was also introduced to Einar, then nineteen years old and a tall, gangly law student. We did not know then how important that young man would be to the future of our family.

In the fall of 1941, we moved back to the Granlis' house and an uneasy coexistence. I suppose that the rent we paid Nils each month was still an incentive for him to try to be civil around us. Alma was always kind and patient, but the tense situation in the household, aggravated by Nils's heavy drinking, took its toll on all of us. Fortunately, I was able to go to school and escape the situation at home every other day. Even Christmas was no longer the same that year. Although we still had plenty of food, rationing of items such as sugar, flour and butter was now in effect, which curtailed Christmas baking. The prolonged

German occupation of Norway, with no end in sight, affected all of us, and no one seemed to be in the mood to celebrate.

By February 1942, it had become obvious to my parents that we would have to find a place of our own to return to in the fall after spending the summer in Buahaugen. By then, when Nils was inebriated, we were really afraid of him and never knew what to expect.

Our stay with the Granlis came to an unexpected and abrupt end. In March 1942, the *lensmann* paid us a visit with some very disturbing news. A German raid of the villages in his district was imminent, and he urged us to leave for Buahaugen immediately. Travelling to Buahaugen at this time of year and with no advanced planning was a terrifying prospect. We did not know how we would manage all by ourselves or how we would get all the necessary provisions. Nils promised to look for someone to bring us what we needed at regular intervals, and we had no choice but to believe him. So on a bright, sunny day, we set out on skis with one of our neighbours, each of us carrying as many supplies as we could.

It took several hours of skiing through deep and heavy snow to reach the *seter*, but since there were four of us, we made deep tracks in the snow. We hardly recognized Buahaugen when we arrived — the landscape looked like it was frozen in time. Our neighbour helped us carry wood inside and start a fire in the fireplace and the stove to warm up the cottage. And then he left. We were all alone in the great expanse of snow and ice.

The brook was frozen, too, except for a small opening, where we were able to fetch drinking water — on skis, of course. When we needed water with which to wash ourselves and our clothes, we melted snow in a large pot. At night, the cottage got freezing cold, and it was usually my mother who got a fire going before my father and I arose in the morning. We could not go outside without putting our skis on. It was almost inconceivable that we could stay here all alone until the farmers came up for the summer. But that was what we did — at least that was what my parents did.

After a few days in the mountains, I did something that was probably the most selfish thing I have ever done in my whole life. My only excuse is that I was only thirteen years old. I told my parents that I wanted to go back to Rogne, to stay with Nils and Alma and to go to school. Their reaction was predictable. I was their only link to the village in the event that something happened to my father, and now I wanted to leave them completely on their own. In the end, they let me go, provided that I agree to return to the mountains every weekend with provisions.

So I set out on my skis, retracing the tracks we had made a few days earlier. I felt free as a bird — for a little while. Then I began to realize that I was now all alone in the great snowy expanse I had to cover. What would happen if I fell and could not get up? It was a frightening thought, one that I had to quickly put out of my mind. Only when I arrived at the bend where the mountains and villages on the other side of the Volbu lake came into view did I feel safe. I still had to ski downhill before I got to the main road, but at least I passed some farms and knew that I was almost at the Granlis' house.

Alma in particular was happy to see me and have me stay with them. I went to school as if everything were normal, but nothing was. The enormity of what I had done weighed heavily on me, and every night I looked up at the sky and in the direction of Buahaugen, wondering and worrying about how my parents were doing. It was a most difficult time for the three of us. Every weekend when I skied back up to the mountains, the loneliness of the slow climb, first through dense snowy woods and then across the wilderness of the higher plateau, almost overwhelmed me. I was also always terrified of what I would find when I arrived in Buahaugen. From one week to the next, I worried that the trail would no longer be visible and that I would have to rely on clearings in the woods and the frozen lakes to guide me.

When I returned years later to Buahaugen with my son, Marvin, and my husband, Stefan, they were incredulous when they saw the distance I had skied all by myself when I was only thirteen years old.

But, although I was nervous and scared at the time, I knew that I was just doing my duty, and every weekend after I had seen my parents and had convinced myself that all was well with them, I was grateful and able to go on for another week. By May, when it had become too difficult to ski because of the spring thaw, I left school and the Granlis and stayed in the *seter* with my parents.

Somehow the spring months of 1942 passed. Difficult as it was to manoeuvre outside wearing skis in March, it became even harder to manage without skis when the snow was melting in May. Instead of skiing, we waded through deep, loose and wet snow. It was almost impossible to carry the buckets of water from the brook up to the cabin. But the spring sun is strong in the mountains, so by the end of May, all the snow had disappeared and life became easier. The recent months had, however, taken their toll. The three of us had suffered a serious setback psychologically, and our nerves were completely on edge. Even when the farmers returned to their *seters*, Buahaugen somehow did not feel the same as in previous years. Perhaps we knew subconsciously that this would be the last summer we would spend in the mountains.

Two people visited us that summer. An engineer from Nordiske arrived with the usual envelope of money and stayed with us for a few days. He urged us to leave Norway as soon as possible because the Germans had begun escalating the persecution of the Jewish population in Oslo, Bergen and Trondheim. My father told him that we had no connections to the Underground in the area, and without their help, we would not be able to escape. The engineer left with the promise that he would do everything in his power to help us.

The second visitor was Einar Wellén, our neighbour's young nephew. He had the same message as the engineer from Nordiske, and when he heard that we were literally trapped in Rogne, he mentioned that he had a friend in the Norwegian Underground. With this friend's help, Einar hoped to help us escape to Sweden.

During the summer, we rented a furnished house on the outskirts of Rogne. Although it should have been a relief to live in larger quarters and on our own, we were too nervous to appreciate it. I could no longer go to school; my parents believed it was too dangerous, and I made no effort to change their minds. We tried to stay as close to the house as possible, and I was the only one in our family who did the necessary shopping. In the winter, when new ration cards were issued, I travelled quite a distance with our *spark* to pick them up. With my heart pounding in my chest, I asked for and received the ration cards.

The engineer from Nordiske appeared one day, delivering the terrible news about the deportation of the Norwegian Jews to concentration camps. He promised to be back in January to fetch us and bring us to safety. We had not heard from Einar in a while. My father's depression and violent outbursts became more frequent. We felt caught in a trap with no way out.

My fourteenth birthday on December 27 was like any other day, and when I complained that we did not even have a small celebration, my father lost his temper. I had never seen him that furious and was really frightened when he lifted up a chair and threw it against the wall. My poor father needed an outlet for his feelings of helplessness and frustration, and my complaints triggered this violent outburst.

We had almost given up hope when in the early morning hours of January 14, 1943, there was a knock on the door. Fearing the worst, I opened the door. Relief surged through me when I recognized Einar Wellén. He was with another young man who turned out to be his friend Arne Myhrvold. Both were exhausted and frozen because they had spent the night travelling, the last part of the journey on an open truck bed. The two young men wasted no time in telling us that everything was arranged for our escape and that we would be leaving early the following morning. They advised us how to dress and what to bring in our knapsacks. What I remember best from that day was standing over a kitchen sink dying my hair blond. Much depended on us and how we would be able to handle the situation. We would travel by truck to a small place near Fagernes, where we would board a train headed for Oslo. We would leave the train in a suburb of Oslo. A minister, recognizable by his clerical collar, would meet us at the station and take us to his home, where we would stay until the next transport to Sweden.

This plan sounded easy enough, but we all knew that danger would be lurking in every corner. The truck could easily be stopped for an inspection, and what was even more likely was that we would be asked for identification papers on the train. But these were risks we had to take to save our lives.

While we were preparing to leave, there was another knock on the door. We stared in disbelief at our new visitors, the engineer from Nordiske with a companion. They, too, had come to rescue us. After some discussion, it was decided that we would follow Einar and Arne's plan, since that seemed to be the better one. Arne had been working in the Norwegian Underground for quite some time and had helped many people cross the border into Sweden via the route we were planning to take. It was quite a coincidence that these two pairs of caring individuals arrived the same day.

We left Rogne at dawn the following day. Our truck made it without incident in time for the train to Oslo. Einar and Arne travelled on the same train as us, but in a different compartment, and in fact we did not see them again. My father hid behind a newspaper, and my mother and I tried to look as relaxed as possible. Not one word was spoken among us. By some miracle, we were not asked for identification papers. When we reached the suburb of Oslo where we were to meet the minister, we got off the train and looked anxiously around. To our immense relief, he drove up immediately in a car, and we were off to the minister's home.

It was a lovely house, a home such as I had not seen in a long time, beautifully furnished with paintings on the wall and a piano in the corner of the living room. Coffee and sandwiches were ready for us, and we were shown to a room to rest. The minister told us that we might have to spend the night there, because there might not be a transport to the border that day. This possible delay made us very nervous, but at the end of the day, a message was received that we should leave immediately.

We were driven by car to a farm and shown into the barn, where some other people were sitting in the hay waiting, including an elderly Jewish woman who had been rescued from a hospital. It was there that we found out that the three of us were among the last Jews to leave Norway. When there were about thirty people in the barn, a truck drove up, and the Jewish woman, my parents and I were told to get in first, closest to the cab. Eventually a tarpaulin was stretched across the truck bed and covered with grass. My father immediately realized that he would not be able to stay in such a confined space because he was extremely claustrophobic. He moved slowly to the other end of the truck, where he could see some light through the slits of the tarpaulin, and disappeared from our view.

This was the ultimate agony. Not having my father close to me during those dangerous hours was unthinkable. I called, "Vati, Vati" many times, but there was no reply. I began to imagine that he had gotten off the truck and had been left behind accidentally. The man next to me told me to be quiet, since the noise I was making would endanger everyone on the transport. I was so nervous and upset that my whole body shook, and I could not keep my teeth from chattering. During the next couple of hours, I hardly thought about the danger we were in. All I could think of was whether my father was on the truck and what we would do if he were not.

Suddenly the truck stopped and so almost did my heart. Loud voices were heard outside, but soon we were on our way again. We all breathed an audible sigh of relief, but not a word was spoken. The next time the truck came to a stop, we were told that this was the end of our drive and that we would have to walk the rest of the way to the

Swedish border. A guide would accompany us. Slowly the truck bed emptied out, and when at last I saw my father and put my hand into his, I was oblivious to the danger we were in. All that mattered was that my father was with us. We walked through the snowy woods, quickly and in absolute silence. Suddenly, a small cabin appeared as if from nowhere with lights blinking through its windows. And then we heard "Welcome to Sweden. Come inside." We then saw the silhouettes of two Swedish soldiers coming toward us.

Our long odyssey, beginning in Oslo on April 8, 1940, had ended.

Life in Sweden

The soldiers' cottage was warm and equipped with several bunks. My parents and I were each assigned to a bunk, after which my father immediately fell into an exhausted sleep. When one of the soldiers wanted to give my father a cup of coffee, I motioned to the soldier not to wake him up. Although I was just as tired as everyone else, I could not fall asleep. Too much had happened in a short time, and it was impossible for me to relax.

The following morning, we were transported to a small city in Sweden called Alingsås, where we were quarantined in an old school. Here we met a few other Jewish people from Oslo who had recently escaped to Sweden, among them Gerd and Charles Philipsohn and their mother. Gerd was a year younger than I and always clinging to her mother's skirts. I also met four Czech girls who had lived in Norway the last few years, been adopted by Norwegians and converted to Christianity. Under Hitler's laws, however, they were still considered Jewish. Not only had they lost their biological parents, they were now separated from their adoptive parents. All they had was one another.

While we were in quarantine, we were allocated some clothing and examined by doctors. The doctor who examined my father was astonished when he saw the small but deep wound on his back and recommended that he be operated on as soon as possible to close the wound.

About two weeks later, we moved to a rooming house in Alingsås. Once again, my parents and I lived in one room. Here we had to share the bathroom and the kitchen with many other people. The two people I remember from this place were *Fröken* (Miss) Potovsky and her mother, who had a different surname. The two were also refugees, but they seemed to have been living at the rooming house for some time. Fröken Potovsky had a piano in her room and played Chopin incessantly — almost from morning till night. Her mother was her greatest admirer and let it be known that her daughter had been a concert pianist in her native country (Poland, I believe). Even today, when I hear Chopin's music, I always think of Fröken Potovsky.

My father decided to heed the doctor's advice and have the surgery he had suggested. The prospect of being operated on in a small town in Sweden, after all he had been through, was extremely stressful for my father. Since my mother would not leave his side during his hospital stay, she could not look after me during that time, so a solution had to be found.

A Jewish orphanage had been established in Alingsås for refugee children who needed a place to stay. I fit into that category, albeit temporarily. Not all the children there had lost their parents, but for many different reasons their parents were unable to look after them. Living with so many children was a new experience for me but one I enjoyed. The atmosphere in the orphanage was cheerful thanks to the leadership of the wonderful person in charge, Nina. Nina had a heart of gold. She scolded when it was warranted, comforted when tears were flowing and intervened when disagreements erupted; in short, she was on the go from morning till night. Nina was a psychologist by profession and herself a refugee.

Most of the children there had come from a Jewish orphanage in Oslo that had been established a few years before the outbreak of the war. When the persecution of the Jews escalated in Germany, some parents chose to part with their children rather than risk their children's lives, and sent them to Norway, where they thought they would be safe. The Oslo Jewish community had supported the or-phanage. After the German occupation of Norway, the Norwegian Underground smuggled the children across the border to Sweden.

Two of the children I remember best are Ruth Elias and Josef Fenster. Ruth was a cute young girl my age who had been sent from Germany to Sweden with her younger brother. After spending sev-eral years in various foster homes, Ruth was sent to the orphanage in Alingsås, while her brother was in a boys' home in a different Swedish town. When I met Ruth, she had gone through so much hardship that she had become a difficult teenager. At times, Nina had to be very strict with her. That same year, when she was only fourteen years old, Ruth began working in a photo shop in Alingsås.

Ruth's parents were deported from Germany to Theresienstadt concentration camp, where her mother remained until she was liber-ated in 1945. Her father had been sent to Auschwitz and died on the transport. When Ruth was reunited with her mother after six years' separation, the two did not get along. Eventually, Ruth met Amek Adler, also a survivor, in Stockholm, and they got married.[2] The two immigrated to Canada more than fifty years ago and live in Toronto. Amek became a successful salesperson; Ruth succeeded in overcom-ing most of her old fears and lives a productive life as a wife, mother and grandmother. We met again one summer after having been out of touch for decades.

Josef Fenster was a quiet boy about my age. Also born in Germany, he was one of the children who had been in the orphanage in Oslo. His parents died in a concentration camp. When the war was over, he returned to Oslo, became a baker and tried to blend into Norwegian Jewish society, which took him many years. Although the Norwegian

---

2   Amek tells his story of surviving through ghettos and concentration camps in his memoir, *Six Lost Years*, published by the Azrieli Foundation in 2017. Amek passed away in 2017.

Jews who had survived the war had been refugees themselves in Sweden, they felt somewhat superior to those whose backgrounds were different from theirs. Josef is one of the most generous people I know. He never married, is now retired and devotes all his free time to the Jewish community. He has become one of its esteemed and prominent members. I have met Josef each time I have visited Norway and saw him last on my visit in 2002.

After my father had his operation, during my visits to the hospital, I was shocked to see him so pale and weak and feared for his future. After a week, he was able to return to the rooming house, but it took five more weeks for him to recover, and the operation had been unsuccessful. When my father was strong enough not to require my mother's constant care, I returned to my parents. I had spent six weeks at the orphanage.

When we arrived in Sweden, the Salomons, who were friends of my parents, had been living in Stockholm for several years and were well established. They had no children. They were originally from Frankfurt am Main, a city close to Wächtersbach. The Jews in Frankfurt were generally Orthodox, and this was the environment Hermann Salomon came from. His marriage to a beautiful non-Jewish divorcee shocked his parents and the whole Frankfurt Jewish community, despite the fact that she converted to Judaism. My father contacted them, and they were so happy to hear from us that soon afterwards they came to Alingsås to see us. Their visit was a shot in the arm for my parents. I was included in the warmth of their reunion, and when the Salomons asked me to call them Onkel and Tante, I readily agreed. I had always been reluctant to make strangers an uncle or an aunt, but the Salomons seemed like family and became Tante Ruth and Onkel Hermann without any reluctance on my part. Before they left, they not only loaned us money but offered to help us with whatever else might become necessary for our relocation in Sweden. They also invited me to come to visit them in Stockholm whenever possible.

My father had advised Nordiske Destillationsverker in Oslo of our safe arrival in Alingsås, and the company suggested that he get in touch with its branch in Malmö, a city located in South Sweden. At the request of the head office, a position was created for my father at Nordiske in that city. After packing up our meagre belongings, we went to Malmö by train, happy to leave Alingsås and the rooming house behind.

It did not take us long to settle in Malmö. We rented a nice, modern one-bedroom apartment in a quiet neighbourhood and bought some second-hand furniture. I was given the small bedroom; my parents slept on a hide-a-bed in the living room. Life assumed some normalcy. My father went to work in the mornings, my mother did the grocery shopping in stores that were new and strange to her and took care of the apartment, and I went to school.

Since I had missed about five months of schooling again and my education in Rogne had left much to be desired, I was quite nervous about starting at yet another school. The Norwegian and Swedish spoken languages (as well as the Danish language) are very similar. The written languages, however, are another matter entirely. Going from Norwegian as it was spoken and written in Oslo to the New Norwegian in Rogne and now to Swedish was not easy. The school in Malmö, to which I was admitted without losing a year, was a vocational high school, where I studied not only the usual subjects but also typing and shorthand. I enjoyed the typing and shorthand lessons. These lessons gave me practical skills to fall back on if needed in the future. One of my teachers, a woman in her fifties, took pity on me and volunteered to tutor me in Swedish. I was soon able to express myself well in Swedish. It did not take long before I caught up with my contemporaries, with even my written Swedish becoming acceptable.

Despite the fact that my father's health was manageable again, I always feared that something would happen to him. The wound on his back opened up again soon after the surgery in Alingsås, and my mother continued to tend to it. She wanted to teach me to cleanse and bandage the wound, but I was too squeamish. Although things were finally going quite well for us, I was always nervous and apprehensive. I suppose the past had caught up with me.

The Jewish community in Malmö was small. Rabbi Berlinger was in charge of the synagogue and the Sunday morning cheder. My Jewish education had been put on hold in April 1940, and it was important to my father that I resume where I had left off. So instead of enjoying some free time on Sundays, I went to cheder. I immediately loved the Jewish environment and felt completely at ease with the other children there. I became friendly with the rabbi's three children: a daughter, Yetta, who was a year older than I, a son exactly my age and a younger daughter. Yetta became my special friend. Often on Shabbat, after attending synagogue, I was invited to the Berlinger home for lunch. Orthodox Judaism held a certain attraction for me, but I never became observant.

Malmö is a port city and has wonderful beaches. The sand is almost white, and the beach is kept spotlessly clean. It was there that I finally learned to swim properly. A long wooden pier led from the beach to two large sea-water swimming pools, which were separated by a wall but not covered. One pool was for men and the other for women, and everyone swam in the nude. Although I was rather shy, I loved the sensation of swimming without a bathing suit and gladly paid the few öre (Swedish pennies) for admission.

It takes about two hours by boat to reach Copenhagen from Malmö, and on a clear day one can see the skyline of Copenhagen from the beaches in Malmö. Knowing that the Germans were in such close proximity always gave me an eerie and unsettled feeling.

A new wave of refugees began to arrive in Malmö, Danish Jews from Copenhagen and its surrounding areas. Most of them had made their escape in Danish fishing boats. The fishermen stowed their Jewish passengers in the holds of their boats and left Denmark under the cover of darkness. Many people were saved in this manner. My parents became friendly with several couples, friendships that in many instances lasted all their lives. Stories were told of the heroism of the Danish people during the German occupation and how the king protected his Jewish citizens. Only a small number of Danish Jews were deported to Theresienstadt concentration camp, of whom very few perished due to the influence and interference of Danish officials.

Returning from the synagogue on a Friday evening, my father brought home a guest. Jack Ganz was a Norwegian Jew, a bachelor in his early forties, a small man with a pronounced nose on his narrow face and an easy, friendly smile. Both my parents enjoyed his company, and he became a steady fixture in our home. He was a helpful and generous person who remained in our lives for years to come.

One day a letter arrived in the mail, addressed to me. To my amazement, it was from Sigmund Meiranovsky. He was in a German prisoner-of-war camp and had obtained his brother John's address in Sweden through the efforts of the Red Cross. John, in turn, had sent Sigmund our address. Now my personal "war effort" began. Many letters between Sigmund and me crossed the ocean, and when we met at the end of the war, he told me that the arrival of a letter from me always made that day a brighter one.

In the spring of 1944, I went to visit John and Beks in Norrköping, Sweden. Beks was pregnant and quite unwell, but we still made the most of the few days we had together. That same spring, I also visited Tante Ruth and Onkel Hermann in Stockholm. Onkel Hermann became my guide. We visited museums and beautiful parks and dined in fancy restaurants, all of which were a novelty for me. Onkel Hermann made a deep impression on me with his knowledge of art and his interest in everything around him. Although older than my father, he appeared much more youthful, and other than my father, he became the most important person in my life for some time to come.

When school was over in the spring of 1944, I decided to make use of my new skills — typing and stenography — and began looking for work. I was certainly not a fast typist and my shorthand left a lot to be desired, so I was overjoyed when I was offered a job in a small office. It turned out that all I had to do was answer an occasional phone call. I was left alone in the little narrow office from the time I arrived in the morning until 4:00 p.m. A typewriter was my only company. Two weeks later, I had to admit to myself that this job was not for me, and I left.

An ad in the newspaper attracted my attention. A small company was looking for an office assistant, and I could not believe my luck when I was hired. The office consisted of only two people, the owner of the company and his secretary. In my opinion, the young secretary was the smartest and most efficient woman I had ever met, and I was completely in awe of her.

Things went really well at the office for a while, until one day I committed a blunder I have never forgotten. I was handed a stack of letters to mail, one of which was a registered letter that had to be taken to the post office. Instead, I mailed all the letters in a mailbox. When I realized what I had done, all I could do was stare at the mailbox, hoping against hope that it would regurgitate the registered letter. I ran back to the office and confessed to my boss what had happened, expecting to be fired on the spot. But he calmly went to the post office, and the letter was retrieved. I became, if possible, even more eager to please, and at the end of the summer I regretfully left the job and the two people who had shown me such kindness and consideration to return to school.

The construction of a beautiful theatre complex had recently been completed in Malmö. I saw my very first play on an outing with my class and loved it. To my great surprise, Yetta's brother asked me one day if I wanted to go with him to a performance of *A Midsummer Night's Dream*. My first date! It was also my last with him.

At the end of 1944, it became obvious that the Germans were losing the war, and by the spring of 1945, it was only a question of time before Hitler would have to capitulate. The Allied forces were beginning to land in Germany, and rumours of concentration camps and atrocities abounded. But nothing could have prepared us for what we were about to witness.

In April 1945, my class was told by the teacher who had tutored me in Swedish that all the students at the school would be relocated for the remainder of the school year and would be going to school in shifts. Our school would be used to house concentration-camp prisoners who would be liberated shortly through the efforts of Sweden's Count Folke Bernadotte. At the same time, the teacher expressed regret that the graduating class would be unnecessarily inconvenienced by this move and said that she found the whole thing grossly unfair. I was shocked. This woman, who I had thought was so kind, had no compassion at all for the unfortunate people who were about to come to Sweden. In anticipation of their arrival, many schools in Malmö were converted into temporary hospitals while the Malmö museum, a reconstructed fort located in a lovely park and surrounded by a moat, was prepared to house the relatively healthy survivors.

And then they started to arrive. The museum was soon filled to capacity with Jewish people of many origins. Few were from Germany. For my parents, it became a daily ritual to go to the museum to make inquiries about our family, but no one had any information. One day, they spoke to a young boy from Cologne. Although conversation across the moat was difficult, my parents learned that he was sixteen years old and the sole survivor of his family, except for an older brother who was in the United States. My father suggested to me that since the boy and I were the same age, it might benefit the boy to have a friend visit him. From then on until the end of the boy's quarantine, I went to see him every day. Even though we had to shout across the moat, we managed to become good friends, and when he was able to leave the museum, he came to our apartment several times before leaving for the United States to join his brother.

Although Sweden had remained neutral during World War II, many Swedes had secretly sided with the Germans. Not so secret were the transports of German weapons and troops that were allowed to go through Sweden. Although the Jewish population in Sweden was negligible, many of the Swedes were antisemites, something I experienced first-hand in a very unpleasant encounter. I was visiting my friend and shouting across the moat in German as usual when a man passed by and yelled at me that I was nothing but a whore. I was in shock and too young to have the presence of mind to react. Now I had one more thing to worry about. Would the man be there the next day? He never came back.

The schools, too, began to fill up. In the schoolyards where kids had been playing until recently, pitiful victims of Hitler's concentration camps walked aimlessly about. The bony hands reaching for the bread and chocolate that people brought them, the emaciated faces staring through the fences and begging for food, the fights among the survivors that sometimes erupted over a piece of bread — it all made me almost physically ill. Yet I returned to these schoolyards every spare minute I had with more bread and chocolate, which turned out to do more harm than good. Soon it became strictly forbidden to bring food from the outside since many of the former prisoners had gotten seriously ill from the unaccustomed caloric intake. They had been starving too long and their digestive systems could handle only small portions of food at one time, with portions now measured by the doctors in charge. I cannot describe the deep sorrow and despair I felt that spring of 1945 and even now, a lifetime later, I can still feel the pain of the sixteen-year-old I was then.

When the survivors were healthy enough, they were released from the various quarantined facilities in Malmö. The majority of them headed for the larger cities in Sweden, such as Stockholm and Gothenburg, in search of work. Eventually, many immigrated to Canada and the United States. I think about how no matter how their lives turned out, the memories of the horrors of the camps would always be with them.

The Germans finally capitulated on May 7, 1945. My parents went out that night to spend the evening with friends, but I was in no mood to celebrate. The events of the past weeks had depressed me so much that all I wanted was to crawl into bed. Since we were living on the ground floor, I had always rolled down my blind before getting undressed. That evening I did not. A face appearing in my window almost paralyzed me. I screamed. He ran away, but he had seen me partially undressed and I felt completely violated. I never told my parents.

The end of World War II signalled the end of our life in Malmö, as well as a new beginning. We had come to Sweden as refugees and could, therefore, only stay as long as there was a need for it. Both Norway and Denmark had been liberated, and all of us who had settled in Sweden during the war had to return to our respective countries.

The good news was that Nordiske in Oslo was anxiously waiting for my father to resume his position as director of its paint division, but the bad news was that the company had been able to find only a small studio apartment for us. That was the best accommodation the company could find under the circumstances. Since we had been living in Malmö for more than two years, my mother, in particular, became busy winding up our affairs. She arranged for our furniture that was to be shipped to Oslo to be placed in storage and packed up our personal belongings. Finally, in the fall of 1945, we said goodbye to all our friends in Sweden and went by train to Oslo, the city we had left so long ago.

Back in Norway

The Germans had left every city and country that they occupied in shambles, Norway among them. It was a shock to come from the peaceful, prosperous small city of Malmö to Oslo, where there was a shortage of everything from food to housing and clothing. Sugar, flour, meat and chocolates were still rationed. The city of Oslo looked drab and neglected, and the shortage of adequate housing was critical.

We moved into our studio apartment, which was not large enough for two people, let alone for three. The living room served as both our bedroom and dining room. My mother could barely turn around in the tiny kitchenette, and before long the three of us thoroughly detested our surroundings. Even my father's health was affected, but it would be a year and a half until we were able to move.

Life had to go on. My father went to work every day at Nordiske, my mother struggled to keep our little place clean and tidy, which was no small feat, and I went to school. This time, though, I did lose a year and was now in Grade 10 instead of Grade 11, which meant that I had three more years of high school to complete. Once again, I had to switch languages. Apart from the language that was spoken and written in the cities, the high school curriculum included two other Norwegian dialects, one that was spoken and written in the countryside, *Nynorsk*, or New Norwegian, which I remembered fairly well from Rogne, and another called *Gammelnorsk*, or Old Norwegian, which was completely unfamiliar to me. Math and *Gammelnorsk* were my nemeses. Another problem was studying in our little apartment, but I somehow muddled through that year.

Beks, John and their little daughter, Renée, as well as Beks's sister Hanna and her eleven-year-old son, Robert, had in the meantime also returned from Sweden. Hanna's husband had perished in Auschwitz. Fortunately, both families were able to return to the apartments they had lived in prior to their escape. John inherited the store his brother Jack had left behind when he and his family were deported to Auschwitz, where they perished. Beks, John and Hanna took over the store, a men's haberdashery, which they called Corner, since it was located on a busy corner in the centre of the city. The three of them worked there tirelessly from morning till night, completely devoted to its success. John was the buyer and looked after the business end, Beks was the salesperson and Hanna did alterations in the downstairs area. A shortage of goods was their main problem, and building up a stock was almost impossible. As quickly as shirts, socks, pants or jackets were delivered, they were snapped up by the customers.

For years to come, Corner would be a landmark in the city, where sailors bought their uniforms and men of all ages knew they would be well served. When Beks retired at the age of seventy, her nephew Robert assumed the responsibilities of running the store, and when he died prematurely in his fifties, his wife took over. The store eventually went downhill, together with the area in which it was located, and it was sold many years later.

Both Beks and John realized how stressful my family's living conditions were, and their home was always open to us. Although Beks was tired from standing on her feet all day in Corner, she served us the most delicious open-faced sandwiches and home-baked cookies, which were a treat during the prevailing food shortage. My father fell in love with little Renée, who was a beautiful child with straight dark hair and huge brown eyes, though she was also quite spoiled. But she was only a baby then, a year and a half old, and she was the apple of John's eye and could do no wrong.

Beks was a slender, attractive woman and just as competent in her home as she was in the store. The apartment was spotlessly clean. When visitors came, no effort was spared and everyone was always welcomed with a smile. John was a handsome man but quite complex. Although much younger than my parents, who had after all been John's parents' friends, John and Beks became our best and closest friends, a friendship that survived time and distance and lasted till the end of their lives.

Sigmund, too, returned to Oslo in the fall of 1945. He had not yet been discharged as an airman, and in his light-blue uniform of the Royal Air Force, he looked absolutely dashing. My heart skipped a beat whenever I saw him, and soon I was head over heels in love with him. All the young Jewish girls competed for his affection, and each time I saw him pay special attention to one of his admirers, I suffered painful pangs of jealousy. Sigmund told me in later years that he was aware of my feelings and did his best to squelch them. To him, I was still his little sister. It took me quite a while to get over this infatuation. Several months later, Sigmund left for the United States where he has lived ever since. He never married.

The Norwegian Jewish community had suffered severe losses during the war. Of the approximately 760 Norwegians who had been deported to Auschwitz, only around twenty-eight survived and returned home. One of these survivors was twenty-four-year-old Kai Feinberg, who also became very popular with the single Jewish girls in Oslo. Although nervous and high-strung, he was a charming, good-looking young man. In time, he would be the leader of the Jewish community in Oslo, a position he held for many years. A book about his imprisonment in Auschwitz was written with his help and published after his death. In 2000, I translated his book, *Prisoner No. 79108 Returns,* from Norwegian to English.

Since the Jewish community felt it could not function without proper leadership, a rabbi and a cantor were hired from abroad. A Jewish youth group was established, which we called *Jødisk*

Ungdomsforening — Jewish Youth Society — and met at regular intervals. Excursions were organized to a community-owned cottage that was located in the mountainous area overlooking the city of Oslo. My old friend Celia and I were usually the youngest in this group, but we always participated in whatever the Jewish Youth Society had to offer.

In the summer of 1946, the first post-war Jewish inter-Scandinavian conference was held, with participants from Norway, Denmark, Sweden and Finland. These conferences, which were held every summer, were run like a camp, but with emphasis on workshops and discussion groups. It was important for us to exchange ideas with contemporaries from the other Scandinavian countries, and the conferences were always very successful. Many a romance blossomed during the two-week conferences, a number of which led to weddings. Although I attended that first conference after the war when I was seventeen years old, I did not seem to fit in. Perhaps I was too young or too shy, or maybe just too serious.

For the young Jewish women in Oslo, these summer conferences were especially important. So many young men had been deported and killed during the war that there was now a real shortage of eligible men. At the conferences, at least there was a chance that the young women might meet someone. When all else failed, the young Jewish women dated non-Jewish men, often resulting in marriage. As for the young Jewish men, they often married Norwegian gentile women, claiming that they knew the Jewish women too well to fall in love with them. Today the Jewish community in Norway consists mainly of intermarried couples. However, more often than not, the Norwegian gentile women convert to Judaism and become Jews in the truest sense of the word. Their children are raised as Jews, and the families attend synagogue on a regular basis.

That same summer, I heard about a private school that offered a one-year course covering the curriculum for the last two years of high school. The fact that I was one year behind in school troubled me a great deal. I was in a hurry to finish school, because I felt that I had to complete at least my high school education while my father was still able to work. His health had deteriorated somewhat during that year, which he attributed to our cramped living conditions, and I was worried. I applied and was accepted. The school was located in an old building on Drammensveien — in fact, everything about it was old, from the creaky stairs leading to the classrooms to the desks and other equipment. There was no schoolyard.

As soon as the school year began, I realized that it would be impossible to study as intensely as I needed to in our one-room apartment. But where could I go? Beks and John quickly found a solution. They approached their friends Klara and Alf Ellingsen and asked them if they would rent us the empty room in their apartment. When the Ellingsens heard of my dilemma, they agreed, and I promised myself that they would not regret their decision. I had dinner with my parents every night, but breakfast and a sandwich for lunch from the Ellingsens was included in the price of the rent.

Klara was a tiny, blue-eyed blond woman. She was very friendly and loved to talk and tell stories. Because I was always so busy, our little get-togethers took place late at night over a snack and a cup of coffee. Her husband, Alf, was her exact opposite — tall and gangly and very quiet. Alf and Klara were the parents of a ten-year-old son, Bjørn-Sverre, a typical Norwegian light-haired, blue-eyed boy, who was tall for his age and quiet like his father. Since his scholastic achievements left much to be desired, I often helped him with his homework.

My room at the Ellingsens' was small and narrow, sparsely furnished with a bed and a desk, and had a window looking out on Bogstadveien. For the next nine months, I divided my time between school, dinner at my parents, an occasional visit with Beks and John and studying in my room at the Ellingsens'. I arose at 5:00 a.m. and studied until late at night. There was no time for any social activities, but I was determined that this would be my last year of high school.

My classmates were a mixed group of people, all older than I, whose schooling had for one reason or another been interrupted by the war. A few young men had been fighting overseas; others had been working in the Norwegian Underground. One young woman who hailed from a small village was absolutely brilliant and astounded all of us with her knowledge. A young man and a young woman discovered each other at the beginning of the school year, fell in love and got married the following year. But as diverse as the students were, we all worked extremely hard. The requirements for obtaining a high school diploma in those days were stringent, the school fees were high and no one could afford to fail.

In the fall of 1946, the owner of a small plumbing company, Mr. Myhrvold (no relation to our rescuer Arne Myhrvold) began building a duplex in a suburb of Oslo. Someone at Nordiske knew of this project and approached Mr. Myhrvold, offering him a large sum of money in exchange for his promise to rent the upper floor of his house to my parents. Offering key money was the only way to get an apartment in those days, and we were very fortunate that the opportunity presented itself. The deal was made, and although my parents had to wait another six months until the completion of their apartment, they knew that their stay in the studio apartment would come to an end in the foreseeable future. I remained with the Ellingsens until the end of the school year because their place was much closer to the school than our new home.

Without Nordiske's help, we would never have been able to rent our beautiful new apartment. In retrospect, however, I realize that the paint formulas my father handed over to Nordiske must have brought the company huge profits.

The apartment was located in one of Oslo's many attractive suburbs, which was reached by commuter train. The station was about a ten-minute walk from our home. Our apartment consisted of a large living-dining room, two bedrooms, a kitchen and a bath. Since the kitchen was too small to accommodate the large refrigerator my parents bought, the refrigerator was placed outside our entrance door on the landing. The view from our balcony off the living-dining room was breathtaking: the whole city of Oslo and the Oslo Fjord beyond lay at our feet.

The furniture my parents had bought in Sweden, as well as the dishes, Persian carpets and paintings they had brought from Germany, came out of storage. Now they were finally put to use. I believe this new home truly rejuvenated my parents. A picture taken in the summer of 1947 shows my smiling father having a "tea party" with his little friend Renée on our balcony.

Onkel Gustav, Tante Selma and Elfriede had settled in Bridgeport, Connecticut, where my aunt's relatives lived. My uncle, a small wiry man, worked as a labourer in a lumberyard. It was a hard life. Gustav had decided early on that if his brother survived the war, he would visit him regardless of the cost. So, in the early spring of 1947, Onkel Gustav arrived in Oslo for an emotional reunion with my parents. Nothing could have touched my father more or given him greater pleasure than this visit with his only surviving brother. He and my mother both knew how much my aunt and uncle had sacrificed to make this trip possible. This was the last time the two brothers met.

That same year, a contingent of about four hundred Jews arrived from Europe at the invitation of the Norwegian government. The goal was to repopulate the Jewish communities that had been nearly destroyed by the Nazis. Little did I know that their arrival would change the entire course of my life — my future husband, Stefan Szilagyi, a survivor from Hungary, was one of the new immigrants. One young couple got married as soon as they set foot on Norwegian soil. Their picture was splashed on the front pages of several newspapers. This couple, Judith and Victor Farkas, would later become dear friends of ours.

The majority of the new immigrants were from Hungary and Poland. Norway was still suffering from the effects of the occupation, and the ongoing housing shortage became a big problem for the new-comers. Some of the families were housed in barracks located on the same commuter line as our new apartment, only a few stations away. The single young men generally found accommodations in rooming houses in Oslo or the smaller cities. Most of the newcomers managed to find jobs in their trades, where they also learned to speak Norwegian. The majority of these newcomers eventually immigrated to Canada and the United States, where the opportunities for a higher standard of living were undeniably better than in Norway.

In the spring of 1947, I took part in Norway's Day of Independence. May 17 is marked with festivities that last from morning till night. In the morning, children of all ages from the schools in Oslo march in a parade on the main street of the city, Karl Johans gate, to the royal castle at the top of the street, where members of the royal family stand on their balcony and wave to their young subjects. The children are dressed in their finest for the occasion, some in the different national costumes of the country, and all wave tiny Norwegian flags. Some of the schools have their own marching bands that proudly precede them.

Of all the different groups represented in this parade, the *russ*, the graduating students, in their red or blue tasselled caps are the most noticeable. The red caps represent the year's graduates of the standard secondary schools and the blue caps the graduates from the business secondary school. They are an exuberant group, singing songs, shouting slogans, waving flags and often riding in old cars that are painted red or blue for the occasion. It is a somewhat strange custom, since none of these students have as yet passed their exams. But this is their day to celebrate, and celebrate they do.

In the spring of 1947, I was part of the noisy gang of *russ*. I proudly marched in the parade in my red dress and my red tasselled cap. Sadly, I found myself feeling like an outsider even on this happy day. In the evening, a class dinner had been arranged in a restaurant, but because we were such a diverse group, we did not have a party afterwards like all the other *russ*. I remember walking down the hill to the commuter train all by myself, feeling both dejected and elated. Yes, I was alone that night, but I had accomplished so much in one year. I was convinced that I would pass all the exams ahead of me. And I did — with flying colours! I applied to the one-year business course offered to high school graduates at the business secondary school and was accepted. Whatever happened, I would have a sound education, and if possible go on to university. My ultimate goal was to be a translator.

During the last few school years, I had learned quite a bit of English, and I had often wished I would have the opportunity to visit England to practise my newly acquired language. In the summer of 1947, my dream came true in the form of a graduation present from my father. On a beautiful day in July, I boarded a Norwegian ship for Liverpool and six weeks of glorious freedom.

The crossing to England was uneventful. I enjoyed the sun and the fresh ocean breeze as the ship made its way across the waves. When we approached Liverpool, I was almost sorry that the voyage had come to an end. From Liverpool, I took a train to Birmingham, where my cousin Erna was waiting for me on the platform with her young son, David, in her arms. We were so happy to be together again after a separation of more than ten years.

Erna and her husband, Erwin, lived in a blue-collar neighbourhood of Birmingham. Row upon row of identical houses had been built in this area, and the Brauners lived in one such small house. Erwin worked in a jewellery factory at a modest salary, but somehow they managed to make ends meet. Erna was busy with David, who was about eight months old at the time, and she was pregnant with her second child.

Erna and I made up for lost time and enjoyed each other's company. We talked, I helped her around the house and we went on walks with the baby. On Fridays, we baked her famous spice cake for the weekend. The days and weeks just flew by. The one thing I did not like about Birmingham was the weather. The sun did not shine more than two days during the several weeks I spent there.

A few weeks after I arrived in England, I went to London. I went sightseeing and visited all the famous buildings and museums I had heard about. The history I had studied in school came alive before my eyes. One afternoon I went to see the film *Gentlemen's Agreement*. I fell in love with Gregory Peck, who played the main character, and stayed in the theatre to see the film a second time.

While still in Oslo, I had contacted a Jewish youth organization in London. Now I phoned one of its leaders and was told that they were going on an excursion to Stratford-on-Avon the following Sunday. Would I like to join? I was glad to have the opportunity to meet with British young people around my age, and on the bus trip to Stratford, I was finally able to try my conversational English (I spoke German with the Brauners). We travelled through the English countryside, which is particularly beautiful in midsummer with its pristine green grass on gentle slopes, and even the weather cooperated. In Stratford-on-Avon, Shakespeare's birthplace, we attended a play, none of which I understood, but it was a thrill just to be there.

When I returned to Birmingham, Erna and I resumed where we had left off, and all too soon it was time to say goodbye. It would be many years until we would meet again.

An End and a Beginning

In the fall of 1947, I once again entered a new school. But this was different — it felt normal. Having applied and been accepted, I was ready to start at the *Handelsgymnasium* (business school). My classmates were all the same age as I, and all of them had graduated from the standard secondary school in the spring that year. The pace was not nearly as frantic there as at the previous year's private school.

That *Handelsgymnasium* was a business school par excellence. Our subjects were varied, and all the classes were geared toward a career in business — Norwegian, English, German and French composition of business letters, Norwegian and English stenography, extensive typing courses and bookkeeping. Since I had always had trouble with numbers, bookkeeping was one subject I came to detest. I had already decided that I would never become a bookkeeper, but since it was an important subject, I still had to devote much time and effort to it.

We had not seen our friend Jack Ganz since we left Malmö and often wondered where he was. So my parents and I were delighted when he turned up one day at our apartment with a young woman. Helena was a concentration camp survivor from Hungary and among those who had been rescued by Count Bernadotte and brought to Sweden. That was where she and Jack had met. From the way the two looked at each other, we knew that Jack had come to introduce us to his future wife.

My parents and I instantly liked Helena. Her open smile, her valiant attempts at speaking a mixture of Swedish and Norwegian, and her warmth made her irresistible. Like so many others, she was all alone in the world, the only survivor of a large family. Somewhat embarrassed, she divulged that she was pregnant. To my surprise my father, who would usually have frowned upon such news, was all smiles. Soon after their visit, Jack and Helena got married, and my mother began knitting baby clothes. Despite the housing short-age, Jack had managed to rent a one-bedroom apartment, and when their first daughter, Irene, was born, their small family was all settled. They would become the parents of two more children, a son, Howard, and another daughter, whose name I cannot recall. Jack and Helena would remain in our lives for years to come.

My family's life was quite stable, with a comfortable routine. My father went to work at Nordiske every day, and my mother took care of our apartment. She was often annoyed with me, rightfully so, be-cause my room was messy. I know now that her frustration with me, as well as my own arguments with her, were quite normal for a par-ent and an eighteen-year-old girl, but at the time the situation made me quite unhappy. Since my mother was often unreasonable in her demands, my father sided with me on many occasions, and peace was restored until the next incident.

One day, my father returned from the office in a particularly good mood. On the train coming home, he had run into Einar Wellén, whom none of us had seen since January 1943, although my father had spoken to him on the phone to thank him for all he had done for us. Einar had told him of his recent marriage and promised to visit us shortly with his wife, Marit.

And then on November 11, 1947, that which I had dreaded almost all my life suddenly happened. It happened on a night when a Women's International Zionist Organization (wizo) meeting was scheduled to take place in the evening with a prominent speaker from Palestine. This was a big event for our small Jewish community, and women of all ages, including my mother and me, flocked to the hall where the meeting was held. I cannot recall another occasion when the two of us went out together at night and left my father alone. We came home around 10:30 p.m. I was already in my room when I heard my mother cry out in panic. I ran into my parents' bedroom. There lay my father on the floor in a pool of blood. With great difficulty, we managed to lift his limp body and put him into his bed, but I think we both realized that we were too late. Traces of blood from the bathroom into the bedroom confirmed that he had felt ill and had been on his way to lie down. He had died all alone, and my mother and I were inconsolable. A doctor came and confirmed what we already knew. Although the doctor assured us repeatedly that even if we had been home, we could not have done anything to save my father, the knowledge that we were not there for him haunted us for months to come. My father's healthy lung had collapsed; it had simply been overworked.

Onkel Hermann arrived from Stockholm the following morning, and the funeral took place the day after on a cold, dark winter day. I was chilled in body and soul and never shed a tear. I did not see anybody and did not hear anything; I wrapped myself in a cloak of silence, from which I emerged only later that night. I suddenly began shaking uncontrollably. I could not breathe and thought I was going to die. A doctor had to be called to give me a sedative. I had had a panic attack.

Onkel Hermann stayed with us another day. I can still see him and my mother sitting at our dining room table discussing our future. He was very concerned about our financial situation, and, as he had done in Alingsås, he offered his help. It was hard for me to understand that he felt it necessary to bring up the subject of money the day after my father had been buried, but the conversation did not have the same effect on my mother. She knew that money might become an issue and had already begun to worry. Even though many people came to visit us during the shiva, the seven days of mourning, our house seemed empty after Onkel Hermann left. He was unable to stay with us longer because Tante Ruth was sick. We found out later that she was seriously ill, suffering from cancer.

After the shiva ended, my mother and I had to pick up the pieces of our lives. It was hard for me, but it must have been so much more difficult for my mother. She had lived with and for my father for nearly twenty-five years and almost her whole raison d'être was gone. The fact that she and I had never been really close further complicated the situation.

My father's colleagues at Nordiske Destillationsverker were shocked when they were told about his sudden death. He had never told anyone about his ongoing health problems. The company offered my mother a lifelong modest pension in exchange for the complete ownership of my father's formulas, which she accepted. This small but steady income, combined with the interest on a small savings account, would at least enable us to make ends meet.

Once again our lives were difficult. An ad in *Aftenposten*, Oslo's principal newspaper, offered a part-time job for a fast typist to type manuscripts. I applied and was hired on the spot. From then on until the end of the school year, I spent every afternoon in the back of the bookstore, typing as fast as I could. (School started at 8:00 a.m. and finished at 2:30 p.m.) My typing improved considerably, and every Friday I was handed an envelope containing my payment, which made it all worthwhile.

My mother spent most days at home and began to do knitting for friends and their families, for which she was paid small amounts of money. Although she had loved to knit, I think she didn't enjoy it now that it was for a different purpose. She was without a doubt very lonely, particularly since I was gone all day and had homework to do when I came home. I did not have much patience for her, and she complained bitterly that I never had time for her. We settled into a strained coexistence.

One day coming home on the train, my mother met Mrs. Gutt-mann, a Hungarian woman who had come to Norway that spring with her husband and two daughters, Susan and Marianne. They lived in a barrack a few stations away from us, and she and my mother promised each other they would stay in touch. Mrs. Guttmann spoke fluent German, and although she was somewhat older than my mother, the two quickly became friends. Both of them were going through hard times, and they found comfort in each other's company.

Since my mother could not bring herself to use the room in which my father had died, we decided to rent it out, which would augment our income. We let it be known in the Jewish community that there was a room for rent in a newly constructed house, and it was not long before we had a call from Dr. Martin Markus, who rented the room for his fiancée, Ruth. Her brief stay in our home benefited all three of us. Ruth was compassionate with my mother, and she became my friend and confidante. When she left to get married, we missed her sorely.

The Guttmann family came one Sunday afternoon for coffee, and that was the first time I met them. Mrs. Guttmann, although younger than her husband, was obviously the spokesperson for her family and the one who gave the orders. Mr. Guttmann, in his late fifties, was a dour-looking man who contributed little to the conversation. Of the two daughters, Susan and Marianne, I immediately liked Susan better, although she was seven years my senior. Marianne was eighteen years old at the time, and she talked about going back to school as soon as her family could afford it, as she hated the radio factory where she was working at the time. Susan, who had been a secretary in Hungary, had already found a similar position in Oslo. She spoke and wrote several languages, and she very quickly mastered the Norwegian language as well. All four of the Guttmanns detested the barrack in which they lived. They had been promised better housing in the not-too-distant future.

On May 17, 1948, I marched again in the students' parade, this time as a *blå russ* (blue graduate), wearing a blue tasselled cap indicating that I would graduate from the business school. Even before graduation, I had interviewed for my first full-time job and had been hired by Ole Bull A/S, a medium-sized structural steel import company. I would be Ole Bull's secretary, taking dictation in Norwegian and English.

The evening before my first day of work, I attended a small party. Drinks were served, and since I was not used to drinking, the alcohol soon had an effect, making me happy and relaxed. When I came home, however, my room seemed to be spinning, and I did not sleep all night. How would I be able to work the next day, my first day on the job? Except for a drop of wine here and there, I have never had a drink since.

I really enjoyed working at this job. Ole Bull was a very pleasant boss, patient and always ready to explain my work to me. It was not long before he had trained me to be the type of secretary he had been looking for. The office hours were from 9:00 a.m. until 4:00 p.m. The rest of the day was mine to do with as I pleased, a luxury I had not enjoyed in years. I began to see friends from the Jewish youth organization and frequently visited our friends the Meierans (formerly the Meiranovskys) with my mother.

Susan Benyovitch (formerly Guttmann) and I took the same train to work every morning, and we became good friends. Little by little, she told me her story. She and her family had lived in hiding in Budapest during the war, thereby avoiding deportation. She had been engaged to be married, but her fiancé had been sent to work camps and then to a concentration camp. He survived, and he and Susan were married in Germany after the war. One year later, they divorced. Susan's husband wanted to live in Palestine, but the Guttmanns, who were not Zionists, claimed that they could not manage without Susan's help. She chose to stay with her parents.

It was around that time that young men finally took some notice of me, and I had a few dates. I met a young gentile Norwegian who was a teacher and a gentle, compassionate person. We went out a few times, but when he asked me to meet his mother, I backed off. I did not need any more complications in my life. I was not a popular girl; I was too shy and serious. I also lacked self-confidence and thought of myself as being unattractive because of my somewhat protruding teeth. I had seen a dentist soon after my family returned from Sweden. The dentist quoted an exorbitant price for new braces and stated that I'd have to wear them for three years. At the age of sixteen this was an eternity, and I refused. Nevertheless, an old photograph of me reveals a smiling, pleasant-looking young girl with brown, wavy hair and a rather nice figure — all in all quite ordinary.

In Norway in 1948, we were still short of almost everything, including clothing and material. I was, however, able to get hold of cloth for two dresses and was soon the proud owner of one beige, brown-trimmed "new look" dress and a brown dress with a fitted waistline. These were the only nice dresses I owned for a long time. I had also splurged on a pair of platform shoes to go with my new outfits. I was ready for bigger things.

In November 1948, the mourning period for my father was over and I was finally able to go to a dance at the Jødisk Ungdomsforening with my friend Celia. Even I had to admit that I looked quite nice in my new dress and my new rimless glasses. When we entered the hall, I noticed a few new faces and assumed that they belonged to some of the new immigrants who had arrived the previous year. I was having a wonderful time with my friends, whom I had not seen much lately, and enjoyed the music and the dancing. Suddenly, a young man I had never seen before stood before me and asked somewhat gruffly, "Do you want to dance?"

Standing before me was a slight young man with an intense face and a head full of curly brown-black hair. He told me his name — Stefan Szilagyi, that he was originally from Budapest and that he was a new immigrant to Norway. That evening he did not leave my side.

and when the music ended, he offered to take me home. I warned him that this would involve a train ride, so he took me to the station instead and promised to call me soon.

And call me he did. For the first time in my life, I was dating someone on a regular basis. In the beginning, I was not quite sure if I liked my new friend, but he was persistent, and I soon came to enjoy his company. We went to films and restaurants, and on Sunday afternoons we often went dancing. Although Stefan had been in Norway for less than two years, he had already been involved in a profitable business venture with Hungary. At the time we met, he was able to afford the kind of entertainment that had always been beyond my reach. My two nice dresses were put to good use.

During the war, Stefan had been in Hungarian forced-labour camps and had spent the final six weeks prior to liberation in Mauthausen concentration camp. There he became seriously ill with typhoid fever but fortunately managed to survive.

When the war was over, Stefan made his way to Budapest, only to find that most of his family had perished. His father had died when Stefan was sixteen years old, and now his mother, too, was gone, along with many other family members. An uncle and an aunt, both on his mother's side, had survived. However, after a brief stay in the city of his birth, Stefan decided that staying in Hungary was out of the question. Antisemitism remained rampant, and he thoroughly hated his surroundings.

Stefan felt he had no choice but to return to Germany, where life was chaotic to say the least, but, along with other young survivors, he made a life for himself. He attended university in a town called Erlangen and lived for a while in a home for elderly people in Nuremberg, Germany. On an errand to Bamberg, he and his friend Otto Moses happened to meet a Polish Jew who had astonishing news: Norway had opened its doors to four hundred displaced persons, and all they needed to do to be considered was to give their names and addresses to the proper authorities. Although this seemed like a big joke to the two young men, they registered and then promptly forgot the whole thing. To their enormous surprise, they were contacted about ten days later and asked to pack for their journey to Norway, a country they knew nothing about.

The winter of 1948–1949 passed quickly. I was attending night school twice a week, learning German and French shorthand, and Stefan often met me after classes for a cup of coffee. Although I was by now head over heels in love with him, I doubted that our relationship would have a future. First, I believed that Stefan did not think about the future, and second and very important, we were so different. We grew up in different countries, spoke a different language in more ways than one and came with different "packages." Stefan's cynical smile often upset me, as did his dark humour, which I could not understand. Yet we kept on seeing each other.

That winter, my mother went to Copenhagen to visit some of the people she had become friendly with in Malmö, and then went on to Stockholm to see Tante Ruth and Onkel Hermann. Tante Ruth was very ill by then and my mother realized that Ruth did not have long to live and that this would be the last time they would see each other. Indeed, Tante Ruth died in May 1949. I took two days off work and arrived in Stockholm in time for the funeral. I cannot describe how sad I was for Onkel Hermann that day. He had neither children nor relatives. I could not imagine what life would be like for him. I would soon find out.

In the meantime, Stefan and I were still a couple. My mother liked him very much, as did Beks and John Meieran and Jack and Helena Ganz. Jack and Helena were now living in their small apartment with their baby daughter, Irene, and in the summer of 1949, they arranged for two little girls from an orphanage in France to spend two months with them despite their cramped living conditions. After visiting them one afternoon with Stefan, I saw Stefan putting something into Helena's apron before we left. He had given her money for the girls even though he had by now spent his windfall and had little money to spare. I was very moved by his generosity, as was Helena.

I can no longer remember exactly why Stefan and I broke up that summer, except that we both realized that the relationship was not going where we wanted it to. We each had our own goals, but they were different and conflicting. To get away from my problems, I attended the yearly Jewish conference, and although I enjoyed it more than I had before, I kept thinking of Stefan and wondering how he was.

My work at Ole Bull A/S was going well, and I was becoming a proficient secretary in the process. I took dictation in Norwegian and English, and although I did not want to leave my present employ any time soon, I kept a lookout in the newspaper for a position where I could make use of my German language skills. But Norwegians were still not interested in doing business with the country that had occupied their own, and such requirements were practically non-existent at the time.

My mother had meanwhile been in constant touch with Onkel Hermann, so I was not surprised when she asked me one day if I would mind if she went away with him to a hotel in the mountains for a few weeks. I was truly happy for her; she needed a vacation in the worst way. What I was not prepared for was a letter I received from my mother soon after their departure telling me that she and Onkel Hermann had decided to get married in December. I was shocked. I had seen the same man at the grave of his wife of more than thirty years, grief-stricken and inconsolable, only two months earlier. How could he decide to get married again so quickly? In less than a minute, my feelings for Onkel Hermann changed completely. I was too young to understand that life goes on; I only knew that I was deeply hurt. My thoughts were completely jumbled. On the one hand, I resented Onkel Hermann's decision, but on the other hand, I had no problem with my mother's. She had been alone for more than a year and a half, and ever since Tante Ruth had died, it had occurred to me that she and Onkel Hermann would eventually marry. But not so soon!

Feeling lonely and abandoned, I read the letter over and over again. Thoughts whirled in my head. I knew that this situation would also drastically change my own life. For one thing, I would have to give up our apartment, since I would not be able to afford it on my own. How would I be able to find a small place to live in light of the continuing severe housing shortage? And although my mother and I were not particularly close, I would certainly miss her company.

A couple of weeks later, the two returned from their vacation. Since he was a sensitive and astute person, Onkel Hermann immediately knew that something was amiss. Exactly what the problem was he did not know. He assured me that, although he was sixteen years older than my mother, he was in perfect health. In case he ever got seriously ill, my mother would not have to become his nurse as he had the means to make alternative arrangements. Always generous, he now proposed to pay the tuition for any university of my choice, be it in Scandinavia or elsewhere in Europe. Should I, however, prefer to live in Stockholm, he would gladly rent a small apartment for me as his own was too small for three people.

If anything, these choices left me more confused than ever. Although my mother's marriage was not imminent, I felt I had some very serious decisions to make, and I became ill thinking about my muddled future. Stefan reappeared one day without knowing anything of what had happened in the interval, but not even his presence could alleviate my depression. I therefore decided to take a few days off work and go somewhere quiet to sort out my feelings. Lillehammer was just such a place. I stayed at a small inn and spent the days roaming in the mountains surrounding the small town sometimes just sitting on a rock and enjoying the scenery below me. It was still warm, and the lovely clean air did wonders for my frayed nerves.

My brief vacation was almost over when Stefan unexpectedly arrived in Lillehammer. He had found out from my mother where I was staying and came to be with me for the last two days before I went back to Oslo. It was then that we both realized that we really did not want to be apart, no matter what. And when Stefan suggested that it might be for the best if we got married, everything fell into place and I was happy to say yes.

My mother, I am sure, breathed a big sigh of relief when we came home and told her our decision. Beks and John were also delighted at the prospect of our marriage, as were our other friends. We bought gold rings, and, as was the custom in Norway, I wore mine on my left hand, signifying that I was engaged. Since our wedding would be very small, there was not much planning to do, and the next few months just flew by. I was happy and could not wait for the day when Stefan and I would not have to say goodbye to each other in the evenings. I wanted to be with him always.

There was one thing Stefan wanted to do before we got married — change his difficult Hungarian name to a name that would be easier to pronounce. Coincidentally, his ancestors' names had been Rosenberg, the same as my family's name, before they changed it to the Hungarian name Szilagyi. It was a standing joke that both of us would change our names when we got married, but we did not know that it was not a simple affair to get rid of one name and adopt another. We were given a book of names that the proper authorities would consider. We chose the name Stagre, only to be refused — not Norwegian enough. We ended up with Stenge (meaning "to close") and today I find it amusing that no one in Israel, where much of my family live, can make sense of this surname. It is also funny that when I am in Norway and, for instance, have to leave a message with my name, I often have to spell it. So much for a simple name in Norway, let alone in Canada or Israel.

As planned, Onkel Hermann and my mother got married early in December 1949 and barely made it back from their honeymoon in time for my and Stefan's wedding on December 22. A snowstorm was raging outside when I arrived at the synagogue with my mother and her new husband. The plan was that Beks and John would pick up Stefan on their way to the wedding ceremony, but the bad weather delayed them so much that my mother began pacing the floor out-side the sanctuary. When the three of them finally arrived about half an hour late, they were upset and nervous. To top it off, Stefan had rented a tuxedo and was visibly uncomfortable in his ill-fitting outfit. In spite of everything, the ceremony eventually began, with John as Stefan's best man and Onkel Hermann and my mother at my side under the chuppah, the wedding canopy. I listened to the chanting of the cantor without really hearing him, but when Stefan put the ring on my finger with a somewhat shaking hand, I knew without a doubt that the two of us were right for each other.

After the ceremony in the synagogue, we all drove to the Hotel Bristol on Karl Johans gate for dinner. We had only about eighteen guests, among them our former tenant, Ruth, who with her husband, Martin Markus, had come to Oslo from Elverum, despite the terrible weather. After the dinner, they offered to drive us to Lillehammer, where we were going to spend our honeymoon and which was on their way home. It was quite a drive. Stefan, who was prone to car sickness, sat in the front with Martin, and I sat in the back with Ruth as we made our way through the snowy landscape with the storm blowing all around us. It was late at night when Ruth and Martin let us off in Lillehammer. Although I spoke to Ruth on the telephone, we never met again.

At the end of our honeymoon, Stefan and I returned to Oslo and began our life together. My mother had not given up the apartment when she learned that we were getting married, nor had she taken any of the furniture to Sweden. With our combined incomes, Stefan and I could well afford the apartment. We felt very lucky. Few young married couples were able to have such a lovely home at the time, and we enjoyed it. Astonishingly, I became a totally compulsive housewife. Gone were the days when my mother scolded me for being messy. This was my home, and everything had to be in order all the time. My cooking left a lot to be desired, but I soon came to like baking, with my mother's recipes as my guide.

Both Stefan and I were very busy. I was still working at Ole Bull A/S, but one hour less a day. Stefan soon became a partner in a business manufacturing and selling first gabardine pants and then ladies' coats. Since there was still a serious shortage of materials, people often lined up in front of the store to buy the coveted goods, and Stefan could not turn out enough merchandise to satisfy the demand. This was his first successful venture as an entrepreneur.

We continued to see a lot of Beks, John and little Renée, whom Stefan adored. He had always loved children and would have liked to start our own family immediately. I held back, however, since I was not ready at all to face the responsibility of caring for a dependent little human being.

Around that time, Einar and Marit Wellén came back into our lives. They were already the parents of little Harald, and now the four of us laid the groundwork for a lifelong friendship.

Since practically everybody in our small Jewish community knew one another, we socialized extensively. I occasionally saw my friend Susan, who had by this time moved with her family to a new housing development on the other side of Oslo. Judith and Victor Farkas, the couple whose picture had graced the newspaper when they got married upon their arrival in Norway, lived in the same area with their young daughter, Susan. Although we did not see them much, we knew about one another.

There were also brief trips to Stockholm to visit my mother and Onkel Hermann. It was obvious that he was totally in love with my mother. She was forty-seven years old at the time, and he was sixty-three. He did everything to make her happy, and he succeeded. At last my mother had the lifestyle that she had enjoyed so many years earlier in Germany. The couple travelled a great deal on business and dined in fine restaurants, and my mother bought beautiful clothes. They had a wonderful relationship.

In 1950, when the Korean War started, it never occurred to me that I would in any way be affected. I have never been very political, but as the war continued, we began to feel somewhat uneasy in Norway, despite the fact that the fighting was so far away. It had been only five years since World War II had ended, and, at the time, people in Europe were afraid of any war regardless of its location.

Those who were most concerned about the war were the immigrants who had come to Norway in 1947. Most of them feared that Europe would be ensnared in a new war. Furthermore, they had no roots yet in Norway, and the majority still struggled with the language and to make ends meet. To the Jewish community, they were the newcomers, and it would literally take a whole generation until they were accepted as equals.

At the end of 1950, it became known that immigration to Canada had become quite easy. All one needed was proof of work there, which could be obtained through the Jewish immigrant societies in Canadian cities. Soon many of the new immigrants prepared to leave. Since this type of exodus is contagious, people who had not considered leaving started to do so. "Immigration fever" spread like wildfire.

When Stefan and I first talked about the possibility of emigrating, too, I did not want to consider it. Norway was my home. I loved the country and its people, despite the fact that, being Jewish, I had always felt like somewhat of an outsider. And who could guarantee that I would ever feel more at home elsewhere?

In the summer of 1950, we went to Denmark on a brief vacation, taking along our bicycles. In Copenhagen, which I remember as a beautiful city with wide tree-lined streets, everyone cycled, from messenger boys to CEOs. What I recall best of that trip is my struggle to keep up with Stefan on my bicycle. The traffic at certain times of the day was so heavy that I could barely see him in front of me, and I was scared of losing him or being toppled over by other cyclists. We visited some of my mother's friends, went to Tivoli Gardens and enjoyed the wonderful Danish food.

Although leaving Norway was only a possibility at the time, the main purpose of our trip was to make some inquiries at the Venezuelan consulate in Copenhagen regarding immigration to Venezuela. We actually had an interview with the consul himself, who incredulously did everything he could to dissuade us from making his country our new home. Although immigration to Venezuela was not difficult, the requirements easily met, we decided against this idea because of the consul's comments.

But immigration fever had gripped us. Stefan felt that business opportunities would be better overseas than in Oslo, and we had also realized that the outlook for a Jewish life in Norway was limited. We wanted our children to grow up in a more Jewish milieu. Paradoxically, even though I was reluctant to leave Norway, I suddenly wanted to leave Europe and move to a place where we would feel completely safe. The Guttmann family had already submitted the necessary documents for immigration to Canada, as had Judith and Victor Farkas. They expected to leave in the summer of 1951.

So after giving it much thought, we, too, applied for an immigration visa to Canada. With the help of the Jewish Immigrant Aid Society in Montreal, Auckie Sanft, a large clothing manufacturer, guaranteed a job for Stefan, and we received our immigration documents in a surprisingly short time.

The next few months were difficult. Our lives in the past year and a half had been so pleasant that I often wondered whether we had made the right decision. But the die was cast. We went to Stockholm to say goodbye to my mother and Onkel Hermann. I am sure it was hard for my mother to have her only daughter move so far away, but Onkel Hermann made the parting easier by promising that she could come and visit us in Canada as often as she liked. We sold most of our furniture, gave up our lovely apartment and said goodbye to our friends. Leaving Beks and John was the most difficult of all. They had been steadfast friends and a part of our lives for so many years, and we had no idea when we would meet again.

Because of the prevailing Norwegian currency restrictions, we were allowed to take only a small amount of money out of the country. We invested the rest of our savings in new living room and bedroom sets. We had kept the dining room set that my parents had shipped from Sweden to Norway, so that, too, was sent in a large container to Canada. Because we had paid for the shipment of the container, the shipping company offered us cheap tickets for the crossing, which we gladly accepted. We would be sailing for about ten days. And that was how, in mid-August 1951, we left Norway for Canada, a strange and far-off country.

Arriving on a New Shore

After a ten-day voyage, during which Stefan was extremely seasick, the first thing we noticed when we stepped onto firm land was the incredible heat and humidity. The city of Montreal seemed to be shrouded in a hazy fog, the likes of which we had never experienced before. We made some inquiries and were given the address of a rooming house on Sherbrooke Street, where we spent the first night. When we woke up the following morning, the heat had not abated, and I realized that the summer clothes I had worn in Oslo would be much too warm for the Montreal summer. Of course Sherbrooke Street looked very different in 1951 than it does today, but we were nevertheless impressed with its width and seemingly never-ending length, all of which was shaded by trees that were still in full bloom.

My mother had given me the address of the son of an old friend of hers, who had been living in Montreal for some time. Leo and his wife, Phyllis, had obviously been notified about our arrival, and when we called them, they immediately invited us to dinner that very night. They lived in an apartment in the downtown area. A bridge table had been placed in the living room and set for four, and we enjoyed a leisurely dinner exchanging information. Phyllis, born in Poland, was a concentration camp survivor. Leo was born in Germany and had come to the United States as a young child in the early 1930s, together with his parents. An engineer by profession, Leo had a well-paid position. The couple was expecting their first child and talked about buying a house. They were helpful in suggesting the areas in Montreal where we should be looking for an apartment.

Since the crate with our furniture had arrived at the same time we did, we went apartment hunting the following morning. Even in Montreal there was a housing shortage at the time, but before long we found a spacious apartment on Côte-St-Luc Road, consisting of a large living and dining room, a well-equipped kitchen and a nice-sized bedroom. After a day or two, our apartment looked like we had lived there for years. The furniture we had brought with us made us feel at home right away, and in this new and strange city, our apartment became our sanctuary.

The Guttmann and the Farkas families had in the meantime also arrived in Montreal. As soon as we could, we visited the Guttmanns, who were living in a large, old apartment on Esplanade Avenue. They were going through a very difficult time. Mr. Guttmann appeared to be ill, and in fact he died just a few weeks later from stomach cancer. Neither Susan nor Marianne was working yet, and when their father passed away, they had no money to pay for the funeral. Initially the family was too proud to ask for assistance, but the circumstances left them no choice. They had come to Canada full of hope for a better life. This tragedy was a major setback for Susan, Marianne and Mrs. Guttmann, one that took them some time to recover from.

Victor and Judy Farkas, their young daughter, Susan, and Victor's mother were living in a small apartment on St. Lawrence Boulevard when we first visited them. Working in his trade as a hat maker, Victor was struggling to make ends meet.

The first priority for Stefan and me was, of course, to find work. In 1951, low-paying jobs were abundant, and Stefan was immediately hired by a clothing manufacturer as a cutter at a weekly wage of twenty-five dollars. I fared somewhat better in a small import-export company, whose owner was also an immigrant. He was willing to pay me forty dollars a week as a starting salary, and I considered myself very lucky, but I soon decided that this place was not for me.

Mr. Bull in Oslo had made me confident of my office skills, so instead of scanning the help-wanted ads in the *Montreal Star*, I decided to place my own ad in the newspaper offering my services as an English and German language stenographer-secretary. To my surprise, I received many replies. One of the companies that phoned me was Grinnell Fire Protection Systems, a branch of which became our tenant many years later.

Picture a young woman in a green print summer dress, with a small white straw hat on her head, wearing white gloves and carrying an umbrella. That was me going for an interview with Mr. Jockelsen at Grinnell. Mr. Jockelsen was a department head, originally from Scotland. He assured me immediately that my lack of Canadian experience did not concern him at all as he had found European girls very efficient. He, too, offered me forty dollars a week as a starting salary, with the promise of a raise as soon as I had become familiar with the work. Office hours were from 8:30 a.m. until 5:00 p.m. Since the office was located on Bélanger Street, a bit far from our home on Côte-St-Luc Road, I would just have to get up earlier in the morning. I had the feeling that it would be great to work for Mr. Jockelsen, and I was so happy that I nearly skipped all the way to the bus. I could not wait to start my new job. In my excitement, I forgot my umbrella.

When I came home with the good news, Stefan put a damper on my enthusiasm. He pointed out that since the job was so far away, I would have to leave too early in the morning and would return home too late at night. I had already accepted the position, and I hated to go back on my word. I suddenly thought of my friend Susan. She was looking for a position where quick advancement was a possibility, and I was sure that Mr. Jockelsen would gladly hire her. A phone call to Susan confirmed that she would get in touch with Mr. Jockelsen. What started out as a forty dollars a week job for her grew into a position as department manager. My umbrella was returned to me, and sometimes Mr. Jockelsen asked Susan about "the girl with the umbrella."

My next interview was at Transocean Trading Company, located in the downtown area. The company was looking for a secretary with German and English shorthand skills, and I met with Mr. Sauerland, one of the CEOs, whom I judged to be in his sixties. Mr. Sauerland conducted the conversation in German, and at one point he asked me about my religion. That was not unusual in those days, and when a call the following day confirmed that I was hired, there was no doubt in my mind that this company was owned by German Jews. Surely no German company would hire a young Jewish woman. I was told that I could start immediately, and that the firm would be moving to Drummond Street in the near future.

Transocean Trading Company was run like a well-oiled machine. I immediately loved my job. Ole Bull A/S in Oslo had been importers of steel, and so was Transocean Trading. I was familiar with the terminology in both English and German, which made my work much easier and impressed Mr. Sauerland. The company's move to Drummond Street caused very little disruption in our work. By then, I had realized that I was working for a German company and that I was the only Jewish person in the office. The principal owner of this company was a man named Stinnes, whose father had owned large metal and iron works in Germany, now defunct as a result of the war. Once I had absorbed these facts, I really did not know what to do. Here I had found the perfect job; in fact, after a few weeks, I had already gotten a five-dollar raise, a fortune in those days. However, I was working for people who might have been part of the Nazi regime. Mr. Sauerland had spent the war years in China, but what about Mr. Stinnes? After struggling with this dilemma for many days, my ambition won out. I wanted to succeed and I was on my way. If I stayed at this company for a few years, I would gain valuable Canadian experience, which would enable me to climb the corporate ladder. So, despite misgivings and a guilty conscience, I stayed.

Leonore Griffin, a Canadian-born girl and a recent graduate of McGill University, also worked in the office of Transocean. She was about my age and became not only my friend but also my mentor. She offered to correct my English letters, and I believe that she taught me the most about the English language. Leonore eventually left Transocean to marry a German doctor, whom she had met through the company, and we lost touch.

Transocean was a busy office with constant phone calls. A young woman operated the switchboard, but when she was away on her lunch hour, the other office workers had to take turns replacing her. This was the task that I dreaded the most. Although my knowledge of English was sufficient in most ways, I was completely tongue-tied on the phone. As well, the intricacies of the switchboard intimidated me, and as long as I worked at Transocean, I was never really comfortable answering the phone.

I had worked at Transocean for more than a year when a new co-worker, an engineer, arrived from Germany. His surname was von Eicken, and his demeanour made me instantly uncomfortable. It was not hard to imagine him wearing the high, black boots of the Nazi regime. Fortunately, I was never asked to do any work for him. However, one day he showed his true colours. I was in Mr. Sauerland's office taking dictation when von Eicken came in and whispered loudly into Mr. Sauerland's ear that a man was asking for him and that he was sure that he (Mr. Sauerland) would not wish to see him. He thought the man was a Jew. I immediately stiffened, and my boss, seeing how upset I was, told me that he had finished and I could leave.

A few days later, I caught von Eicken and said to him, "I was insulted by what you said to Mr. Sauerland the other day. I don't care what you think, but the time when you can say anything you want is over."

He replied that he had not known that I was Jewish. I told him that since I was the only Jewish person in a German company, he had to have known. Angrily he retorted, "Aber er war ja ein dreckiger Jude." (But he was a dirty Jew.) I thought I was going to faint.

Mr. Sauerland had been in his office during this exchange, and he was livid with von Eicken. I told him that I intended to leave the company, but his objections were so sincere that I continued working there for another few months. Von Eicken apologized to me during the Christmas party that year — when he was drunk. A short time later, but for an entirely different reason, I would leave the company.

My cousin Elfriede was our first visitor in Montreal. We had not seen each other since 1940, and now we were grown women. Elfriede still lived with her parents in Bridgeport, Connecticut, and was working in an office.

Our first winter in Montreal was a revelation. Coming from a country like Norway, I thought I knew everything about winter. How wrong I was! My Norwegian winter coat served no purpose in the cold, windy and snowy Canadian winter. In order to brave the elements, I splurged on a coat lined with fake fur and sporting a hood. Even though I was now dressed for the cold, the wind was sometimes so strong that it would penetrate my warmest clothing and make it difficult to walk. But like everything else, the inclement weather conditions became part of the Canadian experience.

Stefan struggled to find a decent job, though this was not the only difficult part of Montreal for him. Since he was prone to motion sickness, the streetcars and buses he had to take to work presented a big problem, the 129 streetcar to Snowdon in particular. He often walked for miles to avoid getting sick. In his search for a career, Stefan bought a valet service that came with a truck. His travel problems were exchanged for difficulties running a business in a strange country, and after a few months, he had to sell the valet service. We bought a small English car with part of our capital, so at least Stefan was now able to get around without public transportation.

Because Stefan now had a car, he was also able to look for different work. A small company hired him to sell the septic tank cleaner for which it was the sales agency. This led him to work for Cuthbert Industries, a large plumbing manufacturing company that was the sole distributor in Canada of the septic tank cleaner Stefan had been selling. This was the opportunity Stefan had been waiting for. Although his salary was still very modest, he felt that he might have a future with this company.

Although Stefan knew how to drive, I did not. On a sunny Sunday afternoon, he set out to teach me. After half an hour, he declared that I would never be a driver, and both of us got out of the car in a huff. I continued to believe he was right until quite a few years later, when the instructor of a driving school proved him wrong.

To augment our income, I began working in a second office on Saturday mornings. Stefan picked me up on Saturdays around noon, and we ate lunch in a Chinese restaurant on St. Lawrence Boulevard. The food was good and inexpensive, and eating there was a nice beginning for the weekend ahead. We often went to the movies at the Monkland Theatre that summer of 1952, which allowed us to see two movies and to cool off in air-conditioned comfort — for the price of only fifty cents each.

In the fall of that year, we went to Bridgeport to visit Tante Selma and Onkel Gustav, where we were introduced to the *I Love Lucy* show on TV. Owning a TV was considered the height of luxury in those days. My uncle was still working at the lumberyard. It was very hard work, but from his earnings, they had bought a small house and their lives were comfortable although modest. The TV was a dream come true for my uncle. Now he could watch the baseball games he loved in the comfort of his home and enjoy many other shows.

From Bridgeport, we went to New York to visit Elfriede and her husband, Erik Bender, a young man from a well-known German Jewish family, whom she married in 1952. Like his father before him, Erik was a butcher, as were two of his three brothers. The three butcher brothers ran a store on St. Nicholas Avenue in New York. Elfriede and Erik's first apartment was within walking distance of the store.

Elfriede had given us instructions on how to get to her home, but the approach to New York was nerve-racking, to say the least. Stefan and I felt like two country bumpkins in a big city.

Elfriede and Erik lived in Manhattan in an older apartment, which was furnished with beautiful solid furniture. This was the first time we met Erik, and I found him friendly. Elfriede was already pregnant with their first child. Since they were both Orthodox, their lives revolved around Erik's work, their extended family and their community.

Despite minor difficulties, and they were indeed minor, we both loved Montreal. Here it did not matter if you spoke English with an accent, since everybody seemed to be from somewhere else and Montreal was a truly cosmopolitan city. Living among Jews as we did was also a novelty. We lived opposite the Shaare Zion synagogue, and our neighbours were mostly Jewish. And when we first visited Judith and Victor Farkas on St. Lawrence Boulevard, I was shocked to see that most of the storefronts had Hebrew lettering and that groups of Hasidic Jews were walking on the streets of an area that appeared to be completely Jewish. I had never seen anything like this.

During the first two years we were in Canada, our friends were mostly immigrants like ourselves. In time our circle of friends grew, but most of them were originally from Hungary. We met and became friends with Huguette and Bandi early on. Bandi had gone to the same school as Stefan and had gone to France after the war. There he met Huguette, who was Parisian but had lived in the States for a while. The English spoken by our Hungarian friends was far from fluent, and whenever we got together, Bandi and Stefan spoke almost exclusively in Hungarian. Since Huguette and I didn't understand Hungarian, this presented a huge problem for both of us and forged a strong bond between us. Even though our personalities were vastly different, our friendship endured for nearly thirty years. When a business deal involving Stefan and Bandi went sour, so did our friendship. This incident taught us a hard and painful lesson.

We also became friends with Sanyi (Alex) and Vera Bernstein. Sanyi and Stefan had gone to the same school, lived in the same building in Budapest and been best friends. When Stefan found out that Sanyi was living in Montreal, he was overjoyed. It was not long before the two got in touch and a visit to the Bernstein family was arranged. Sanyi and Vera were the parents of an adorable eight-month-old girl named Vivian. Sanyi's mother, who had also known Stefan, was living with them at the time. She took care of Vivian while the parents worked.

We saw a lot of Sanyi and Vera and became close friends and also met other friends through them. In the summer of 1953, we went on a vacation together to Magog in the Eastern Townships, where Huguette and Bandi also joined us. We stayed at a small inn. The men played tennis, and we all swam in beautiful Lake Memphramagog and got tanned by the warm sun. A photo of that time shows Sanyi and Stefan goofing around, pretending to be cavemen. We all loved and took care of Vivian, who was passed around like a little doll. Those are wonderful memories. Unfortunately for us, Vera felt that she needed to escape the Canadian winters and live in a warm climate. Vera, Sanyi and Vivian left for Los Angeles in 1960.

∼

If my letters did not convince my mother that we were doing well in Montreal, her visit in 1952 certainly did. On the occasion of her fiftieth birthday, Onkel Hermann surprised her with airline tickets to Montreal. Although my relationship with my mother had been somewhat strained in the past, both Stefan and I were as happy to see her as she was to see us. We spent a couple of pleasant weeks together, during which Stefan and I showed my mother the city and its surroundings in our free time. My mother looked wonderful and was obviously very happy in her second marriage.

Then tragedy struck once again. Onkel Hermann, who had been in excellent health all his life, suddenly became ill and was diagnosed with liver cancer. Fortunately, he did not suffer for long and died three months later at the end of 1953. I was distraught. We were so far away, and my mother had to deal with Onkel Hermann's illness and death all by herself. She had lost her second husband, and I could not even imagine the pain she had to endure.

Many letters crossed the ocean in the months following Onkel Hermann's death. He had left a lucrative business behind, and my mother suggested that we leave Montreal and come to live in Stockholm. Stefan could continue the Salomon business, which would provide us all with a good living. Since my mother was the only heir, Onkel Hermann had left her well provided for, and she promised to help us in every way she could.

As tempting as the financial aspect of such a move was, it was pity for my mother that ultimately made us decide to move to Stockholm. I felt in my heart that we were doing the wrong thing by going back to Europe. It was not often in my life that I felt strongly that I did not want to do something but then did it anyway for a variety of reasons.

We sold our furniture, gave up our apartment and our jobs. Mr. Sauerland assured me that Transocean would welcome me back any time, but I knew then that I would not take advantage of his offer. We said goodbye to all our friends and flew to Stockholm in September 1953.

The time we spent in Sweden seems like a dream today, perhaps because Stefan and I were both so unhappy. Since there was a housing shortage in Stockholm, too, we had to live with my mother in her small apartment. Stefan tried to familiarize himself with Onkel Hermann's business but found that he was not interested in the sale of custom jewellery, of which he knew nothing at all. I was completely at loose ends, since I had been working for several years and did not know what to do with all the time I had on my hands. We met old friends, such as Ruth from my time in Alingsås, who was married to Amek Adler now, as well as Yetta Berlinger, my friend from Malmö, who was married to Kuba, and pregnant with her first child. Like Amek, Kuba was a survivor originally from Poland, and the two were friends.

It did not take me long to realize that my instincts had been right
— we should never have come to Stockholm. But how could we return to Canada now? Stefan had given up the best job he had had
there, and we had no home to go back to. In many ways, we were
worse off now than when we had originally immigrated to Montreal.
I felt trapped and deeply unhappy. And in the middle of this emotional turmoil, I decided to become pregnant. Perhaps I thought this
would lend some normalcy to our situation. The pregnancy ended
in a painful miscarriage at the Karolinska Institutet in Stockholm.
Nothing seemed to be going right, and, for both Stefan and me, the
time for decisions had come.

Soon after returning from the hospital, I told my mother that
despite the difficulties we would be facing, we were going back to
Canada. However, I suggested to her that she should think very seriously about coming to live in Montreal, where I felt that she, too,
would be able to start a new life. She would have no financial problems, and, since she was a friendly and outgoing person, she would in
all likelihood have a large circle of friends in no time at all.

So it was decided. Stefan wrote a letter to his boss at Cuthbert
Industries to find out whether his job was still available, and, to his
surprise, the answer was yes. This improved our outlook considerably. Before leaving Stockholm, my mother handed us a cheque with
which to start our lives for the second time in Montreal. With mixed
feelings, we left her alone again and flew back to Canada at the beginning of 1954.

Parenthood

Stefan and I returned to Montreal from Stockholm in February 1954. It was very different this time around. The city was familiar, we had friends here and we were both happy to be back. The first thing we did was rent a one-bedroom apartment in a new building on Goyer Street. Then we bought furniture and a car with the money my mother had given to us in Stockholm. From the beginning, this apartment seemed like a temporary home. I missed the familiar furnishings from our place on Côte-St-Luc Road. The new furniture had no past, and since I have always been a creature of habit, it never really felt like mine as long as we owned it.

This time, Stefan was the lucky one. He began working again at Cuthbert Industries as soon as he could, while I had some difficulty finding suitable work. There was no shortage of secretarial positions available, but one that required knowledge of German was then non-existent. I filled in an application at a large steel company in downtown Montreal. The company asked for the applicant's maiden name. Even though I fulfilled all the requirements, I did not get the job, which convinced me that the name Rosenberg prevented me from getting hired. Eventually, I accepted a job at Goodfellow Lumber Yard, but it was just that, a job. I did not like the atmosphere at the company and decided that I would leave as soon as something better came along. In a way it did — I discovered that I was pregnant again. Stefan was very happy at the prospect of becoming a father; I, on the other hand, was beset by doubts. What kind of mother would I make? I was actually afraid of the added responsibility looming on the horizon and was anxious throughout most of my pregnancy.

To save some money for the arrival of our baby, I had planned to work as long as I could, but it turned out differently. Just a few weeks after I began working at Goodfellow, my doctor told me that to avoid another miscarriage I had to rest a lot, which meant the end of my career at the lumberyard. I had never been able to take it easy, and I was totally frustrated. Time hung heavily on my hands, and I ate more than I should have, thereby gaining too much weight. When I was in my fifth month of pregnancy, I saw a small ad in the newspaper. A builder was looking for a part-time typist. I was given an address on Kent Street, and once I found the street with its beautiful, large duplexes, I realized that this office was in a private home.

It did not take long for Henry, the builder, to decide — I was hired to start working immediately. Even though my work was far from interesting, my surroundings certainly were. I was installed, with a typewriter, at a beautiful dining room table over which hung a splendid chandelier. The room was spacious and furnished in excellent taste. It was obvious that the family was well-to-do, although they appeared to have been in this country for only a short time. Henry's wife, who was also pregnant, came in to say hello and mentioned that she was having a difficult pregnancy. The couple already had a seven-year-old boy. I worked for Henry for about two months. A few years later, we would meet again at a golf club where we had all become members.

When I was in the seventh month of my pregnancy, Stefan and I moved again, since we needed an additional room for the baby. We ended up on the third floor of a walk-up on Ridgevale Street, which was the best we could do on only one income. The building and our apartment were totally unappealing and a far cry from the comfort of our first Côte-St-Luc Road home. I realized soon that I would not be able to clean up the dirt and grime that had been left over from the previous tenants and scrutinized the newspaper. An ad promoted the services of a European woman, and that was how Mrs. Hellermann came into our lives.

It turned out that Mrs. Hellermann spoke German and was a recent immigrant from a town on the Hungarian-German border. When she saw the condition of the apartment, she mentioned casually that the previous tenants had probably been Jews. I was shocked, and I told her that if she did not want to work for Jews, she had better leave right away. Embarrassed, she assured me that this was not the case. Mrs. Hellermann provided us with trusted help for thirty-six years.

In order to get to the second bedroom, the baby's room, one had to go through the kitchen with its ugly brown linoleum. Although this floor covering was the bane of my existence, we never did anything to change it. The apartment also had a spacious living room, a master bedroom and one bathroom. Once again, I felt that this would only be a temporary home until we could afford something better. I kept the place neat and clean and, after climbing the three rather dingy flights of stairs, I was always happy to be back in my own home.

In the meantime, my mother decided to join us in Canada. It had become too lonely for her in Stockholm, and the prospect of becoming a grandmother sealed the deal for her. Because we felt that she should be close to us in the beginning, we rented an apartment for her on Ridgevale Street opposite our building.

Judith and Victor Farkas and their family had also moved to Ridgevale Street. Judith had had a second baby, a cute little girl by the name of Sheila. One day she asked me if I would stay with the baby for a couple of hours, since she had to take her older daughter to the doctor. Sheila was about a year and a half at the time. I agreed even though I had never felt confident with babies. Judith, of course, had no idea that I would find it stressful to take care of Sheila for a few hours, but, despite my misgivings, everything went well. An older child was less of a problem for me, and my neighbour Mary on Ridgevale sometimes left her four-year-old daughter, Ricky, in my care for a couple of hours, which I never minded.

Throughout my entire pregnancy, Stefan talked about the son we were going to have, and as I came closer to my due date, this began to make me more and more nervous. I kept telling him that there was just as much chance that we would have a little girl, but he was adamant. When I was in my eighth month, I looked like a veritable barrel on two legs. I felt heavy and unattractive and could hardly wait for the day that I would give birth.

My mother arrived in Montreal toward the end of my pregnancy. It must have been incredibly difficult for her to wind up all her affairs in Stockholm and take care of all the details connected with such a move. But she had always been a strong woman. Once she arrived in Montreal, she was determined to make a life for herself independent of ours. She joined an ORT (Organization through Rehabilitation and Training) group, where she met women of German origin, and she bought a car and started to play bridge again. And, of course, she anxiously awaited the birth of her first grandchild.

My big day arrived at the beginning of December, three weeks before my due date. The circumstances under which women gave birth in the 1950s differ considerably from those of today. The cheerful hospital rooms, husbands present throughout the whole labour and delivery, holding their wife's hand and wiping her brow and coaching her through the last stage, relatives coming and going — none of these things were done in those days. The lonely, very prolonged labour with impersonal nurses looking in on me occasionally and the last stages of the delivery when I was put to sleep briefly were an ordeal that I have never forgotten.

I did not quite realize that I had become the mother of a son until I was back in my room. Stefan was overjoyed of course — he had been right all along. When I heard that the baby weighed only five pounds six ounces, I became instantly nervous. The pediatrician, Dr.

Doubilet, came and assured me that my baby was fine, but I was not convinced. My roommate had a girl who weighed ten pounds, and she looked like a giant next to my baby. After a couple of days, my little boy became jaundiced, and we were unsure if the *brit milah* (circumcision) could take place on time. I was frantic with worry. I could neither eat nor sleep and lost whatever weight was left over from the pregnancy even before I left the hospital.

But the baby was circumcised on time and was named Marvin after Stefan's father, Martin, and my father, Markus. A nurse, Mrs. Christie, had been hired in advance to take care of the baby for two weeks. As I had anticipated, I was petrified of the responsibility of caring for this tiny new baby. After the first two weeks, my mother paid the nurse to stay for a third week when she saw the stress I was under. But when the three weeks were over, I was still a nervous wreck and told Stefan I wanted to go to work and keep the nurse to take care of Marvin. Totally unsympathetic, Stefan told me in no uncertain terms that Marvin was *my* baby and I had to take care of him. And so I became a mother.

It did not take long before I became totally wrapped up in the care of our baby. Since I have always been somewhat compulsive, Marvin had to be fed at certain hours, changed at regular intervals and bathed at the same time every night. I found the routine difficult because there was no real end to the day during the first months, but Stefan often got up at night to feed and change the baby, and at times my mother also lent a helping hand by spending the night with her grandson.

I had always known that Stefan would be a wonderful father, but of course I could not have known the extent of his total devotion to our baby. He fed him, burped him, changed him and bathed him, and nothing was ever too much. When Marvin rewarded our efforts with his first toothless smile, we were both overjoyed. Marvin's first outing when he was six weeks old was an event. Stefan came home for lunch just to get him properly dressed and installed in his beautiful new baby carriage. It was a balmy winter day in February, and we both joyfully pushed the carriage. From that day on, Marvin had his daily outings, weather permitting. In no time, he became a plump little boy who loved his meals and his bottle — almost unrecognizable from the scrawny baby I had brought home from the hospital.

Shortly after Marvin was born, Mr. Cohen, Stefan's boss at Cuthbert Industries, informed him that his business had taken a turn for the worse and that all his employees would have to take a cut in salary. As we could barely manage on our one income as it was, Stefan decided to leave Cuthbert and devote all his time to the real estate business, which a friend had introduced him to previously through property auctions. Since he knew nothing about this business, he did what he had done in Norway: he used the knowledge of others to inform himself. By visiting many real estate agents in the city, he gradually came to understand the different facets of the business. When soon thereafter he made a $5,000 profit on the quick sale of an old property he had purchased on Wilder Street, we were elated. From then on, our income came in spurts, and since I was used to living on steady salaries, I felt very insecure with this new way of life for quite some time.

We had been married for five happy years before Marvin was born. With his arrival, something gradually changed in our relationship. We were parents and at times forgot about our relationship to each other. Stefan was busy laying the groundwork for our future, and I was then mainly interested in our home. As I had always done, I still continued paying all the bills, typing out the cheques on my typewriter, but apart from that, I was not much help in Stefan's endeavours. Besides working hard, Stefan took French lessons twice a week in the evening from Madame Lette, a recent immigrant from France, and eventually spoke and read French fluently.

In 1955, Stefan built and sold his first apartment building on Bedford Road. The venture was a huge success, and, to celebrate, we went to Florida for the first time that winter. Although Mrs. Christie and my mother took good care of Marvin, he was very unhappy without his parents. During a telephone conversation, my mother told us that he sat for hours in the corner by the entrance door to the apartment to wait for us, which of course made us feel terribly guilty. It was not the most successful trip for other reasons, too. Florida in December is usually cool, and it was absolutely cold that winter. For some summer weather, we drove to Key West in our rental car. After a few days there, we became restless and drove all the way up north to Jacksonville to visit my cousin Erna and her family, who had immigrated to the United States in the early 1950s. We went to the lovely beaches of that city and froze some more.

Erna and Erwin's lives were easier in Jacksonville than they had been in Birmingham. Erwin worked in his métier, window dressing; he had learned window dressing and sign painting in Germany, and now he was finally able to put his profession to use. He and Erna lived in a comfortable house with their sons, David and Paul, and enjoyed the beaches, particularly in the spring and summer.

In the early part of 1956, Stefan began building three triplexes on Bedford Road, one of which would be ours. I was very excited about the prospect of moving from our rented apartment on Ridgevale to our own home. The triplex would consist of a large downstairs apartment, where we would live, and two smaller apartments upstairs, one of which would be my mother's, and a small basement apartment. The other upstairs apartment would be rented out, as would the basement apartment.

By the time we moved to Bedford Road in the summer of 1956, I was pregnant again. The new baby was due in January 1957, so I had plenty of time to get settled in our new home. I loved the big apartment, which consisted of a large living-dining room, a big kitchen, two bathrooms and three bedrooms, one of which Stefan used as his office. We refurnished our living-dining room with black lacquered furniture and a sofa, and curtains were made to measure; I felt that I was at home at last.

Marvin grew into a sturdy little boy, whom Stefan called "Chief." He was a somewhat shy child who started talking only after he was two years old. Apart from suffering from frequent colds that would sometimes turn into croup and give us a scare, he was in good health and had a huge appetite.

I was looking forward to the birth of our second child. Gone were the fear and apprehension that accompanied my first pregnancy. I knew that I would not have any trouble taking care of a newborn baby, and I had no qualms about looking after two children. However, we had decided that this baby, whether a girl or a boy, would be our last.

A few weeks before my due date, I began having labour pains and actually checked into the hospital twice, only to be told to go back home and wait some more. But on January 21, 1957, I was sure that the birth of the baby was imminent. Marvin's delivery had been long and drawn out, but this one was fast and furious. Since the doctor had expected a repeat performance from my last labour and delivery, he was not even in the hospital when I was practically ready to give birth. A nurse was assigned to stay with me — she sat on a chair next to my bed reading a magazine. Such a scene would be unthinkable today, and even then I thought her behaviour was terribly callous. The doctor made it just in time to deliver the baby, and, because I was fully awake this time, I heard him say, "It is a girl!" I was so astounded that I asked him if he was sure. I simply could not believe that my wish had come true.

My hospital roommate was a young Finnish woman who had given birth to a little girl the day before. She told me later that when I was wheeled into the room, the place lit up. I was absolutely euphoric, and as tired as I was, I could not get to sleep. January 21, 1957, was the happiest day of my life. Stefan and I decided to call our little girl Helen, after his mother. When Marvin first laid eyes on his little sister, he was not impressed. "Take her upstairs to Omi" was all he said, referring to my mother. Like Marvin, Helen was also very small when she was born, a few ounces heavier than he had been because she was a full-term baby. And like Marvin, she was cared for by Mrs. Christie. A crib and a folding cot had been set up in Stefan's office. As soon as little Helen would sleep through the night, she would share her brother's room.

From day one, Helen did not have the voracious appetite that Marvin had always displayed, and it took a long time to feed her. At first, the formula did not agree with her, so she did not gain any weight, which of course worried us a lot. Eventually Dr. Doubilet suggested a less rich formula, and Helen began thriving. Mrs. Christie was let go after two weeks; in fact, I could hardly wait for her to leave. Standing over my little girl's crib and seeing her excitement and smiles when she saw one of us tore at my heartstrings. Frankly, I did not think there was a cuter baby to be found anywhere. I called her *Lieschen* — though I will never know why.

Stefan was a very cautious businessperson. He never took any chances and took his time with each new venture. I had become used to being married to someone whose income was sporadic. We lived well, and because Stefan had always been a most generous person, I never had to ask him when I wanted to buy something for myself. He would have liked me to help him with his office work, but I was not anxious to work for him. I was afraid that our relationship would suffer because I knew that our work habits were very different. I was a stickler for details while he saw the whole picture and did not care about the little things. Besides, with two small children, I was a busy mother, and we did not even have an office just then. But no matter how busy Stefan was, he was always home for dinner and then it was his time with the children. He had so much patience. He played with them, he talked to them and he was absolutely the best daddy any child could have.

We began taking the kids on short outings, to parks in the area and Granby Zoo. I have always loved going to the zoo, and these little trips liberated me from the endless routines I had imposed upon myself. On Sunday nights, we often went to Carmen Restaurant, a Hungarian place where the food was delicious. And there were visits to friends who had children the same age as ours. Marvin was always shy and cautious, and although Helen was somewhat more outgoing, she always stayed in close proximity to her brother. Stefan also took "Chief" along on errands, and both of them enjoyed their time alone without the "girls." Marvin was always his daddy's son and very close to him, even to this day.

I made some attempts at going back to work, but the venture was far from successful. Mrs. Hellermann now came to help out twice a week, and as soon as she came in the door, I left for my assignment from Office Overload. I loved the variety of work that came my way as temporary office help, but in the end I got stuck in one place. The boss of that place would call Office Overload over and over again and ask for me. I didn't work there for very long.

My mother had bought a car, and when she was away on trips, which happened quite often, the car stood idle in our garage. Because I did not know how to drive, Stefan often had to take time off work to drive me places with the children. He began to urge me to take driving lessons, so at the age of thirty, I finally learned to drive. My mother's car was automatic, and I loved the independence my new skill gave me. The only trouble was that the car was not mine, and when my mother returned from her trips, she of course laid claim to it whenever she needed it, and that was nearly every day.

We had lived on Bedford Road for about two years when we realized that the quiet street we had originally moved to had become a busy thoroughfare. I sometimes thought that a move to a quiet street would be a solution, but I really did not want to leave my home on Bedford Road any time soon.

In 1959, to get away from our busy street, we rented a cottage in Rawdon, Quebec, for the summer months. Stefan came out to join us at least twice a week. I never liked to be away from Stefan. I felt insecure dealing with the children's health problems on my own, but the fact that Marvin had so many allergies persuaded me that the fresh, clean country air would be better for him than the stagnant heat in the city. My own concerns had to be secondary.

Our cottage was part of the Hollinger Estate, which consisted of several cottages located in a large clearing surrounded by a wooded area. The other cottages were occupied by other families with children. For the kids, it was a real paradise. They were safe everywhere, and every cottage was theirs. The mothers also had a wonderful vacation. On really hot days, we took the children to nearby waterfalls and sat beneath the cascading water to cool off. When Stefan came to the cottage, we cooked hotdogs and hamburgers on the barbecue and had young guests in abundance. It was a delightful summer, although Marvin's wheezing continued in the country, most likely because of all the grass and trees there that bloomed at different times.

In the fall that year, Stefan met Ernest through a business connection. Ernest told Stefan in passing that he and his family were just about to move to their new house in the Town of Mount Royal and that their house in Ville St-Laurent was for sale. Shortly thereafter, we were invited to their new home, and this is when Cila, Ernest's wife, and I first met. We became lifelong friends.

Cila was a petite, slim young woman whose smile did not come easily. She was about my age, born in Poland and a Holocaust survivor. After the war, she had made aliyah to Israel, where she met Ernest. Ernest was born in Czechoslovakia and had spent the war years first in the British army and then in the Haganah. The couple had met and married in Israel and were now the parents of a little boy, Dani, who was four years old.

Ernest proudly showed us their beautiful home on Normandie Drive. The house had a large basement, where the children played while the parents got better acquainted. Stefan voiced an interest in their house in St-Laurent, and Ernest suggested that we could perhaps somehow exchange our house on Bedford Road for theirs on Vincent Street. Stefan was immediately interested. He had recently bought land in Ville St-Laurent and was in the process of building his first apartment building on Gold Street. Living in the area would be a definite advantage.

We visited 2110 Vincent Street soon afterwards. Cila, who accompanied us, told us that she had not really wanted to move from this house. She had been very happy there, since her neighbours were her friends and the house had certainly been big enough for her small family. But Ernest had wanted bigger and better things — hence the house in the Town of Mount Royal, which was built according to his own plans and specifications.

Vincent Street was (and still is) a one-way, crescent-shaped street. The house at 2110 was as if made-to-measure for us. I was excited at the possibility of moving there. Not only did the house appeal to me, but so did the quiet street with its mostly new homes and newly planted trees alongside the road. Stefan and I went home to talk it over and decided that if an agreement could be reached with Ernest, we would move to St-Laurent as soon as possible. Indeed, a deal was struck and the two properties changed hands.

Since we were moving to the suburbs, we thought that I should have my own car. To make up for this rather large expense, I would drive the children to school rather than having them take the school bus. There was some discussion about buying a used car, but in the end we decided to buy a small new car. I have had many cars since that first blue Ford Anglia, but none was ever as treasured as my very first car. I was now completely independent.

My mother was not happy to relocate once again, but since she wanted to be near us, she moved to a new apartment on Gold Street, one of Stefan's buildings, as soon as it was completed. We were then only a five-minute drive from each other.

For weeks prior to the move, I loaded up the trunk of the Anglia every afternoon with our belongings, and, with the children in the backseat, I drove to Vincent Street and put everything we had with us in its place. On the weekends, Stefan moved the heavier things, and slowly but surely we transferred most of our belongings this way. All that was left for the movers on moving day was to move our furniture to our new place. And then we were all set — for what turned out to be twenty years.

Family Life

Once we were settled in our new home, I began to have a real sense of permanency such as I had never had before. Even on Bedford Road, I had always known that we would have to move again sooner or later because we did not have separate bedrooms for the children. But now we had it all, including a beautiful office downstairs for Stefan. In years to come, I would often dream about having to leave this house and would wake up in a sweat. Over time, we made many improvements to our home, which made it even more dear to me.

That fall, Helen started nursery school at the "Y," and Marvin went to kindergarten at Talmud Torah School in Saint-Laurent. It was hard to leave my little girl in a stranger's care — for both of us. But the teacher, Mr. Segal, soon put Helen at ease. When I picked her up a few hours later, she was all smiles, and my own separation anxieties evaporated, too, in no time.

Now that I had a few hours to call my own, as well as a room in our basement that could easily be converted into an office, the time seemed ripe for me to start working for Stefan, as he had asked me to do many times before. I still had misgivings and would have preferred to work part-time elsewhere, but I did not seem to have much of a choice. Stefan wanted me to be at home to take care of the children after school, besides which it was I who picked them up.

We acquired a used desk and office chair. I already owned a typewriter, and we bought an adding machine and a used filing cabinet. My office was ready. It was not exactly the office I had dreamt about at the *Handelsgymnasium* in Oslo; in fact, neither the work nor my surroundings came anywhere near my original plans. Stefan had started to rent out the apartments on Gold Street, and my work consisted mainly of typing rent statements and doing minor bookkeeping. As his workload grew, so did mine. Later I typed listings, which were the bane of my existence. For each property for sale, there were several listings at different times, depending on the circumstances, and all the details had to be typed over and over again. And I, who had decided in school that I would never work with numbers, did little else.

I soon got used to my new routine, and I came to like the idea that I was contributing something to our business while still being able to come and go as I pleased. I joined a Hadassah chapter, a branch of a Jewish women's organization, whose members were young women like me. Since we were all busy during the day, we met every second week in the evening. Most of our programs concerned Israel and the planning of fundraising events for Israeli institutions that urgently needed financial help. I also spent a lot of time on my hobby — knitting.

Early on in our marriage, Stefan introduced me to classical music, but it took several years before I, too, developed a liking for concerts. He often listened to music on the radio or played his records, and in time I began to recognize the works of the old masters such as Beethoven, Tchaikovsky and Liszt. When Place des Arts, the Montreal concert hall, opened its doors in 1963, we bought season tickets and attended many wonderful concerts.

I had many girlfriends then and craved their company. I was open, friendly and always willing to lend a helping hand. Stefan was more reserved and not always in favour of those friendships. Maybe he felt that I was too involved or that I paid more attention to my friends than to him. That may have been true at certain times.

People said I was well organized, but I know that I was rather compulsive. Everything had to have a time and a place. Supper was at 6:00 p.m. every night, and no one ever missed it. No matter how busy Stefan was, he made sure that he was at home before supper. Then he sat in the den with the kids and watched their favourite TV shows, and their howls of laughter reached me in the kitchen while I was putting the finishing touches on supper. My mother often joined us, and on Sundays in the summer when we had our traditional barbecues, there was often a friend or two enjoying a hotdog with us.

We became very friendly with Cila and Ernest, so much so that we spent almost every Sunday afternoon and part of the evening together. The children played in the basement either at their home or ours, and then we all had dinner together. Cila was by far the better cook, but we did not compete. In later years, we played bridge together, and both families enjoyed these afternoons. Once the children got bigger, their interests changed, and eventually, like everything else, our common Sunday afternoons were a thing of the past. Cila, Ernest and Dani moved to Ottawa and eventually to Toronto. Cila and Ernest divorced, but I still saw Cila whenever the opportunity presented itself, either in Montreal, Toronto or Florida.

After Christmas in 1960, we left the children in the care of Mrs. Hellermann and my mother and went on our first trip to Israel. Since Helen and Marvin got along well, they also had each other, and we felt fairly sure that they would not miss us too much. It was a long flight with a stop in Gander, Newfoundland, and absolute torture for me because of my terrible fear of flying. I did not relax for a minute, could neither sleep nor eat and worried about every little sound on the airplane.

Israel was an experience like no other. We had booked a bus tour of the country, and together with about thirty people, most of whom were Americans, we experienced Israel for the first time. Our guide was a young Belgian Jew who had made aliyah a few years earlier, but he knew every stone and bend of the territory we covered and proudly told us the country's history.

My feelings on travelling through this country, which I, as a Jew, was allowed to call my own, were terribly mixed. I felt that I did not have the right to call Israel *my* country, since I had not contributed in any way toward its existence. I also felt like the complete stranger I was because I did not understand a word of Hebrew, which made me feel inferior and inept. I never lost this feeling of inadequacy, no matter how many times I have been to Israel. I was extremely impressed with the accomplishments of the Israelis, many of whom were my contemporaries, who were also survivors of the Holocaust. I felt guilty because I lived a good and easy life in Canada while my fellow Jews in Israel struggled so that Israel would be allowed to exist and be a haven for all Jews. Yet when Stefan suggested that we should perhaps move to Israel, I was horrified. I simply could not leave the home I loved and uproot myself again.

Our travelling companions were a mixed group. An elderly Christian German couple had somehow landed in this entirely Jewish English-speaking group, and their presence was frowned upon by the others. One day, a verbal fight broke out between one of the Americans and the German man, and our guide had to intervene. When the Germans had language problems, I sometimes acted as the translator. In a way, I felt sorry for them.

Yad Vashem, the World Holocaust Remembrance Center in Jerusalem, was not then what it is today. It consisted of only what is now called the Hall of Remembrance, where the eternal flame was already burning in memory of the six million Jews who were murdered during the Holocaust. One corner of the room was occupied by a pile of children's shoes, another by a pile of women's hair. The sight of this reminder of the horrors of the Holocaust brought tears to my eyes. But for some of the Americans, the visit to Yad Vashem was completely meaningless, as I understood from conversations that subsequently took place. The guide overheard some of the remarks and simply shook his head in disgust.

We visited Kibbutz HaZore'a, where my cousin Walter and his wife, Hagit, showed us around. This kibbutz is one of the oldest in Israel, and Walter was one of its original settlers. He has since died, but the kibbutz still exists as a lasting reminder of the courage and persistence of a handful of young German Jews who sought their future in Palestine. In Tel Aviv, we attended a concert and visited a distant cousin of my mother's and some people from Stefan's past. It was a memorable and thought-provoking trip that left me pensive for months to come.

In the summer of 1961, Beks and Renée arrived from Norway on their way to Cleveland, Ohio, to visit John's brother Eli. John had died very suddenly the year before, in his early fifties. Renée had been very close to her father, and his death had left her devastated and rebellious. The purpose of this trip was to relax and to try to recover somewhat from the ordeal of John's illness and death. Stefan, my mother and I showed our special friends around Montreal, drove them up to the Laurentien Mountains and introduced them to Canadian restaurants — we made the most of the few days they spent with us.

⁓

As Helen grew older, I never quite got over the feeling of wonderment at being the mother of a little girl. From the very beginning, I resolved that the relationship between my daughter and me would never be anything like the relationship between my mother and me. When my mother came to Canada, I had hoped that we would magically become close, but unfortunately that did not happen. Now that I was a grown woman with children of my own, we did not argue as we had done during my youth. Thankfully, she had her own life, but she expected me to carry out her wishes at a moment's notice. If I ignored her wishes, she felt insulted and became upset with me, as she did if I did not phone her daily. Stefan was a very good son-in-law, and the two got along well. My mother travelled a great deal in those days, and each time she returned, I childishly hoped that somehow the trip had changed her. It never did.

My mother was intelligent, courageous, optimistic — and selfish. If and when a problem arose, she would say, "Das wird auch schon vorbeigehen" (This, too, will pass). Strangely enough, she spoke to Helen in the same manner as she had spoken to me when I was young, always in a somewhat critical tone. She also once told me that Helen would "sich ausmausern" (become prettier) when I thought she was already the cutest little girl who walked the earth. I did not take this remark too kindly. My mother seemed to feel closer to Marvin, and, as the years went by, the bond between them became even stronger. Helen, on the other hand, was never that close to her Omi. What a pity; they both missed out on so much.

~

Stefan and I tried to get away together once every winter when we could. He still had an aunt and an uncle living in Hungary, whom he had not seen since shortly after the war ended. I, myself, had not been to Norway since we left in 1951 and was longing to go back. Consequently, we decided that we would visit Morocco together to enjoy some warm weather and then go on to different destinations, Stefan to Budapest and I to Oslo. Leaving the children with Mrs. Hellermann and my mother, we departed for Casablanca right after Christmas 1962.

As always, I hated the flight and was relieved when we landed in Casablanca. We immediately boarded a train to Marrakesh. Even the train ride was an adventure. We stopped at many small villages on the way. Women in *abayat* (robe-like dresses) and men in colourful shirts and Arab headdress were waiting on the platform, many of them carrying assorted livestock in cages. They were obviously headed for Marrakesh and its big market.

On arrival in that famous and populous Moroccan city, we were whisked to our hotel by taxi, via sandy roads crowded with people. Our hotel, La Mamounia, was surrounded by a big wall, and once we entered through the gate, we were in a different world. The luxury and beauty of the building and its surrounding garden were an almost unbelievable contrast to what we had seen on our way to the hotel. The garden, which was tropical, lush and green with flowers in abundance, surrounded a huge swimming pool. The interior of La Mamounia was also different from anything we had seen before, its opulent design of Moorish origin. Once back in Casablanca, we visited the souk (open marketplace) and met some of the few remaining Jews of Morocco.

When Stefan and I said goodbye to each other before boarding our respective planes, he said his now memorable line, "I will see you at Marvin's bar mitzvah." Since Marvin was only eight years old at the time, we had a good laugh, but mine was nervous laughter. It was the first time Stefan would be returning to Hungary after leaving the country in 1945, and I was worried about his safety. I reminded him for the umpteenth time to send me a telegram when he arrived at his aunt's house in Budapest, and he gave me his promise.

From Fornebu Airport in Oslo, I took a taxi to Beks's house. Her apartment had not changed in the years I had been away, but without John it seemed empty. Renée was not at home, and I did not see her on this trip. I told Beks about the telegram I was expecting from Stefan, but when we finally went to bed that night, I still had not heard from him. Beks had a grandfather clock that chimed every half-hour, and that night I barely slept. Every half-hour I was up, and every hour I called the telegraph office to find out if a telegram had arrived. By morning, the switchboard operator at that office recognized my voice and said, "Sorry, Mrs. Stenge; no telegram yet." I was frantic by the time Stefan called me mid-morning but very relieved when I heard that all was well. He was scheduled to return to Montreal the same day as I.

I loved being in Oslo again, and after a day or two I spoke Norwegian as though I had never left. What surprised me the most during this visit, and something I had completely forgotten, was how dark it is there in the winter. One day I went out at 9:30 in the morning, and it was pitch dark; by 4:00 in the afternoon, it was dark again. During the few days I spent there on that trip, the sun never shone, and although the climate in Montreal is colder than in Oslo, the winter in Norway seemed more severe because of the lack of natural light.

On my flight back to Montreal, I amazingly was not nervous at all — for the first time in my life. Why was that? I asked myself, and then realized that my anxiety had always been due to the fact that Stefan and I were travelling on the same plane. What would happen to our children in the event of a plane crash? On the other hand, once our children reached an age when they could take care of themselves, my fear of flying together with Stefan became a thing of the past.

The children were disappointed when I came home without Daddy, but I assured them that he would be home a little later. He was not. When he did not arrive the following day, I was frantic. A call to the travel agent produced no results, and I had no idea where to turn. Two sleepless nights later and on the third day, there was a call from Stefan. Would I pick him up at Dorval Airport? He had been delayed by fog in Europe and had asked Sabena airlines to send me a telegram, which they had not done. I must admit that I had almost believed that his joke at Paris Orly Airport about not seeing each other again until Marvin's bar mitzvah would come true.

When they were very young, Marvin and Helen got along extremely well, with Marvin always looking out for her. As they grew older, they often squabbled but no more than most siblings. Stefan continued to be an excellent father. He would take Marvin to the driving range to hit golf balls, and when he discovered how much Helen liked pony rides, he found places to take her riding. For Stefan, the kids came first and he spared no effort on their behalf.

We had been forewarned that sending our children to a religious Jewish school would create a conflict between what they saw at home and what they learned in school. Although nothing could induce Stefan and me to become religious, we always observed the holidays: Rosh Hashanah, Yom Kippur and Pesach. Since we were such a small family, we usually celebrated Pesach with friends, either at their house or ours. Once we even travelled to New York to spend Pesach with my cousin Elfriede and her family.

Marvin became greatly influenced by the teachings of his Hebrew teachers. Several of them were Israelis, some of them Canadians and one, Mr. Goldstein, was originally from Poland and a Holocaust survivor. Of all the teachers, it was Mr. Goldstein who wielded his influence most widely, so much so in fact that some of the parents objected that he was too religious for the school. He taught Grades 2 and 6, and by the time Marvin had finished the latter, he had already begun going to synagogue by himself every Shabbat. Rabbi Halpern at the Beth Ora synagogue noticed Marvin's steady presence at his services and introduced him to the leader of the Junior Congregation, Ralph. The rabbi often invited Marvin for dinner on Friday nights and holidays. Helen was only marginally influenced by Mr. Goldstein's lessons.

In the meantime, the workload in my basement office kept growing, and I often compared myself to a piece of furniture that is shuttled between the upstairs and the downstairs of a house. However, the arrangement was convenient. My life was complete; I was busy and content.

Venturing Out of the Nest

The year 1967 was eventful. The Six-Day War, a conflict between Israel and the neighbouring states of Egypt, Jordan and Syria, had been fought victoriously, and Jews everywhere were rejoicing. This would be the beginning of a lasting peace in Israel — or so we thought. Fortunately, we cannot look into the future, and the present victory gave us all renewed hope for the country that had become the backbone of Jewry all over the world.

Expo '67 was a huge success, and, like all Montrealers, we visited the marvellous exposition many times. My mother turned sixty-five years old in 1967. She had had a few minor car accidents, and when we took her out to dinner on her birthday, we suggested that it might be for the best if she gave up driving and took taxis instead. To my great surprise, she did not object. Thinking about this today, it is hard for me to understand why she so readily agreed to give up the convenience of driving. She sold her car and began to take taxis. I often offered to drive her to appointments and to meet friends, which in retrospect I realize was a mistake, since it encouraged her dependency on me from then on.

It was also the year of Marvin's bar mitzvah, which he considered an important occasion. For him, the religious significance of the event played a major role, and his preparations for the big day took precedence over his schoolwork. I often heard him singing his

Haftorah in his room, so I was confident that he was well prepared when the day of the big event arrived.

Elfriede and Erik, with their children, Sandy and Sidney, came from New York, as did my Tante Selma. Stefan and I had decided early on that Marvin's bar mitzvah celebration would be a modest event, so we hosted a luncheon at the synagogue for our relatives and Marvin's and our friends. I have always thought that there is something touching about a bar mitzvah. For me, the chanting of the boys, who are usually still small and immature, is very moving, and the thought that they are to be considered men in the Jewish tradition seems incongruous.

As time went by, my children's lives went in different directions. Marvin became more religious, and Helen's interest in horses and other animals — which she had acquired from her experiences at her first summer at day camp — grew. She had never really played with dolls and did not like to wear dresses. As she got a bit older, she often stated that she preferred animals to people. Yet she got along well in camp, as well as in school, and always had enough friends to satisfy her needs.

~

Marvin spent the summer of 1970 at Camp Ramah in Ontario, which had an excellent reputation. It was a Conservative Jewish camp with a good Jewish educational program. He enjoyed everything about this camp, and by the time he came home, he had decided that he would go on his first trip to Israel with the camp the following summer.

Around the year 2000, I attended some lectures in Jewish studies in Florida and found out that our excellent professor, Dr. Gittelson, had spent several summers at Camp Ramah in Ontario. Marvin actually remembered him well, and at the end of one of the lectures, I handed the professor a brief note from my son. Dr. Gittelson was thrilled to learn that one of the campers remembered him after so many years, and he told me that the note had made his day.

While Marvin was away that summer, I bought new dishes and separated them into two groups, one for dairy and one for meat. I could not run the risk that my son would one day refuse to eat the food I had cooked because it was not kosher. I have never regretted the decision I made that year.

When Helen was about fourteen years old, we bought her a horse called Maybelle. Owning a horse of her own was a dream come true for our daughter. By this time, we were quite aware of what this decision would entail: we would have to pay a stable to board the horse, we might have veterinary expenses and we would have to drive Helen to the horse on weekends. We knew that we could trust her implicitly with taking care of the horse and acting in a responsible manner. Marvin had had his bar mitzvah and this would be her coming-of-age present, since in those days very few people celebrated the bat mitzvah of their daughters.

Maybelle was a small ordinary-looking horse and quickly became Helen's pet. Horse and rider became very attached. It did not take long before Helen claimed that Maybelle recognized her when she arrived at the stable bringing carrots and sugar cubes. Maybelle accompanied Helen to a riding camp on the south shore of Montreal that summer. Some time later, Maybelle had to be euthanized because she was suffering from equine infectious anemia, a fatal and very infectious disease attacking some horses. Maybelle was followed by Pride, a grey-and-black speckled horse, much larger than her predecessor, which in turn was followed by Ebony, a fine-boned black horse that had been a racehorse.

It was mainly I who drove Helen to the stable, but I enjoyed these occasions to spend time with my daughter. She competed in horse shows, which I attended, primarily because I wanted to make sure that she was all right. My heart nearly jumped out of my chest each time she approached a jump, and when the horse refused, I felt even worse.

As Marvin had forewarned us, he went to Israel with Camp Ramah in the summer of 1971. A postcard we received from him told the tale: "This is my country. It is here I want to live." Although he was only sixteen years old at the time, I did not take this statement lightly. I believed what he said, but he was still very young and I thought he might change his mind in the coming years.

That summer, Stefan and I joined an American Express tour to Europe. It was one of those trips that took you to several countries in a very short time, one day here, the next day there. We had chosen this particular tour because it took us through Cologne. Neither of us really wanted to spend even one night in Germany, but Stefan thought that this would be a good opportunity for him to see where I had lived and for me to visit my childhood home.

We spent only one night at an inn on the Rhine. I remember that when I asked in German for a comforter because it was very cool, the owner of the inn complimented me on my German and asked me if I was German. No, I said in no uncertain terms, I was Canadian. The following day, a sightseeing boat took us to Cologne past castles and large estates to the tunes of "Ich weiss nicht was soll das bedeuten" ("I Do Not Know What That Means") and other German *Lieder* (songs), which nearly brought tears to my eyes. What did this mean? Why was I so moved? I disliked everything about Germany, I did not want to be there and yet a few sentimental songs had me almost crying.

While the others in our group had lunch and visited the Koelner Dom, or Cologne Cathedral, Stefan and I took a taxi to Marienburger Strasse 52, my father's dream house. The street was still lined with trees and beautiful, just as I remembered it, and so was the exterior of the house. I rang the bell at the gate, and a woman opened the door. I told her in German that I had lived in this house many years before and that I lived in Canada now. I asked her if she would mind if we came in and looked at the house. She said she would not mind; she was only the house-sitter while the owners were in America. She was under the mistaken impression that we were friends of the owners, and I did not correct her.

My childhood home was still a beautiful house. The rooms were smaller than I remembered, and the garden with the fountain where my father and I had loved to walk, and which I had thought to be almost as large as a park, was in fact just a small garden. But the fountain was still there. The rose bushes I remembered were gone and so was the dog kennel adjoining the house. But my memories were those of the little girl who had sat on the bench in the garden with her Vati, and they had little to do with today's reality. It is always hard to go back, yet I was happy that I did so in the company of the person closest to me, someone who understood my conflicting emotions. When we returned to the bus, our travel companions had heard from the guide where we had been while they visited the cathedral. Their reaction was touching. Sandwiches had been prepared for us, and the empathy was palpable.

Marvin returned from Israel a full-fledged Zionist, and to this day he has never veered from that course. That fall he became the new leader of the Beth Ora Junior Congregation, a position he filled with much enthusiasm. Tragically, Rabbi Halpern died suddenly that year from a heart attack. The congregation was shocked. The very popular rabbi had been only forty-two years old.

Stefan had started building commercial buildings in St-Laurent. The success of the first property at the corner of Côte-Vertu and Beaulac streets was a long time coming, but Stefan was as always patient, and eventually the building was fully rented. A new and smaller building was constructed next to the existing one, where he built a comfortable office for us, consisting of a reception area that led into his office, with a door between the two, and a third room where we kept our files. The move from my basement office to a *real* office was exciting for me. I felt it gave me a more professional aura, and although our tenants never knew that I was their landlord's wife, I eventually became known, much to my delight, as the owner's efficient secretary.

That same year, we celebrated my mother's seventieth birthday. She had been talking about moving to the King David, a seniors' residence, but I kept dissuading her because I realized she would be even less physically active there than if she stayed in her own home. Over the years, my mother had developed a back problem that made it hard for her to walk, and she was already using a cane. From that time on she had dinner with us almost every night. Either Stefan or I would pick her up and take her back home again. It was only when she spent the afternoon and evening with friends that she did not come to our house in the late afternoon. This was a burden that I took upon myself, and she never resisted. Had Stefan been less understanding, he could have objected to my mother's steady presence, but he never did. We continued this routine until my mother eventually moved to the King David when she was seventy-five years old.

In the fall of 1973, Marvin started McGill University. Just before the High Holidays, he contracted mononucleosis. Because of his allergies, his bout with this illness was particularly severe, and it was quite some time until he recovered. On Yom Kippur, he was still in bed when Stefan and I heard the news on TV about the outbreak of war in Israel. Marvin's radio was on that entire day in spite of the holiday and for the next few days as well.

By the time the war was over, Marvin had made up his mind: he would go to Israel to do volunteer work as long as there was a need. We did little to change his mind. He managed to finish the semester at school, and in January 1974 he left for Israel, where he was to work at Kibbutz Tirat Zvi, a Modern Orthodox agricultural kibbutz near Beit Shean in northern Israel.

With Marvin gone, our house felt empty and we missed him terribly. We had, however, promised to visit him, and just before Pesach 1974, Helen, Stefan and I travelled to Israel. Marvin came to Tel Aviv to spend the holiday with us at our hotel. Then we joined yet another bus tour of Israel to give Helen the opportunity to see this beautiful and varied country.

A visit to Tirat Zvi was mandatory, of course. Marvin seemed to be very much at home and proudly showed us around. Originally founded by Central- and Eastern-European Jews, the kibbutz was already an old and well-established enterprise. We met the kibbutz parents he had been assigned to, as well as various other people. Marvin's work consisted mainly of picking olives. Today he cannot bear even the sight of this fruit.

When Marvin returned from Israel in the spring of that year, he decided to spend the summer working on a project he had started in Quebec City in 1974. To facilitate his work and also to make travelling between home and Quebec City easier, we bought him a small brown Toyota with a clutch. Both children had in the meantime learned to drive, and for a short while, the three of us had shared my car. That summer Helen stayed in town, working at a Coles bookstore. I had for a long time wanted to revisit Norway, and the fact that both children were close to home convinced me that this was the right time to leave my husband for two weeks. In the nearly twenty-five years we had been married, we had never been apart that long.

My Return to Norway

The big day of my departure arrived. Stefan, who had been very supportive about my trip, appeared to have second thoughts, but now it was too late to change my plans. Flying was no longer a problem for me. Stefan and I had done so much of it that I was totally relaxed. In fact, I enjoyed the rush the takeoff gave me. (It actually still does.)

In Amsterdam, while waiting for the Scandinavian Airlines plane, I heard people speak Norwegian and became really excited. Onboard the plane to Oslo, I talked to the woman in the seat next to mine, and although I felt that my Norwegian was somewhat rusty, I was able to communicate.

As on my previous visit, I stayed with Beks. Despite the fact that we had not seen each other in many years, we resumed our friendship where we had left off. It was wonderful to have a friend who was part of my past and who was as interested in my family as I was in hers. Beks had retired from her store two years earlier at age seventy and was now enjoying the free time she had never had before.

That first evening, Beks had invited my old friend Josef Fenster, the boy I had met in Alingsås so many years ago, as well as her sister Hannah for dinner. By the time the guests left, I no longer knew if I was speaking English or Norwegian. It had been a long day.

The following morning, I went to a travel agency on the main street, Karl Johans gate. I scrutinized the pamphlets for different tours of Norway and bought a ticket for a five-day bus tour to the city of Bergen and the fjords, where I had never been before. Before I left on my trip, I called Einar Wellén's office and was told that Einar was at the seashore with his family. I had been in touch with him only sporadically since leaving Norway. Now I was determined to at least speak to him, so I called him at his cottage in Nevlunghavn in southern Norway. He seemed thrilled at hearing my voice and invited me immediately to come visit him and his family in Nevlunghavn. We agreed on a date a few days after my return from my trip to the fjords.

The tour bus I travelled on had English-speaking tourists. Our guide was a twenty-four-year-old Norwegian student, Anne-Marie, whose English was impeccable. By that time, I was completely fluent in Norwegian again and decided to let Anne-Marie know that I spoke her language. She was truly shocked, and subsequently we had many conversations in Norwegian. I don't think she had ever had a tourist quite like me, a non-Norwegian who spoke Norwegian perfectly. Because her father had worked in the Norwegian Underground during the war, it was easy for her to relate to my story of the past.

It is impossible to describe the beauty of the Norwegian fjords, the deep still waters edged by high mountains that seemingly climb out of the fjords. Incredibly, there are farms that can be reached only by boat nestled into the mountains, a sight that is etched into my memory. On one of the boats crossing the fjords, Anne-Marie introduced me to the captain, who told me that his vessel had once been a library boat, distributing books to the farmers in the area.

Anne-Marie had brought some tapes of music by the Norwegian composer Edvard Grieg. The bus left the Sognefjord to the tune of the mighty "Bryllupsdag på Troldhaugen" ("Wedding Day at Troldhaugen") and climbed through mountainous, narrow and curvy roads up to the famous Stalheim Hotel with its magnificent view of the valley below. Although years have gone by since I visited this area of Norway, I still vividly remember its outstanding beauty.

On the morning of the last day of the tour, the guide, Anne-Marie, told us that we would have lunch in Fagernes. This was something I had not been prepared for, but I immediately decided that while the rest of the group was having lunch, I would somehow get to Rogne and back. I hoped to see Alma Granli, with whom my family had lived so many years ago. As soon as the bus stopped, I ran into the only hotel and asked for a taxi, but was told that there were none available that day. I was upset and told the receptionist that I had to get to Rogne and the reason why. A woman standing next to me was so moved by my story that she offered to drive me. In the end, her teenagers drove me. As we came closer to Rogne, they kept asking me if I knew how far we still had to go, but all I could tell them was that the house faced the Volbu lake.

I recognized the green house with its steep approach and ran up the hill. Outside the house, an elderly woman came to meet me. Knowing immediately that she was Alma and not wanting to shock her, I simply asked, "Do you remember a family that lived here during the war?"

She looked at me and, with tears filling her eyes, she said, "You are not Margrit Rosenberg, are you?"

That made me cry, too, and we embraced each other, barely able to speak. In the few minutes I was able to spend with Alma, I found out that Nils had died a few years earlier. Her daughter, who had been a little girl when I lived there, also came out of the house and was quickly told who I was. And then I had to leave. Two teenagers were waiting in the car, and a busload of people were waiting in Fagernes. What a day this had been! That was the last time I saw Alma.

My five-day excursion ended on a high note, and I felt sad that it was all over. But I still had something special to look forward to — the visit with Marit and Einar Wellén in Nevlunghavn.

When the train arrived in Larvik, a small town close to Nevlunghavn, Marit and Einar were standing on the platform. Although it had been years since we had last met, I would have recognized them anywhere. We drove to their beachfront cottage, where Marit served lunch and we talked of everything that had happened in the intervening years. It was a lovely warm day, and in the afternoon Einar took me in one of his boats out to sea, where we went swimming in the cool water. I had never been in this part of Norway before and marvelled at the contrast between the scenery of southern Norway, with its coast dotted with grassy *holms* (small islands) and reefs, and western Norway, with its fjords and high mountains. Marit's twin sister, Lita, and her family came visiting later that day. They owned a cottage close by. I loved being a part of this close-knit family even for a short twenty-four hours. The warmth with which I was treated, the interest they showed in me, my family and my life in general, was something I have never been able to forget. My visit to Nevlunghavn revived and strengthened an old friendship, which has endured until today.

Back in Oslo, I went to see my old friend Celia. She and her family lived in a comfortable house in the suburbs of Oslo. Her eighteen-year-old daughter, Monika, was playing the piano as I came in, but I did not meet her son, Thomas, who was fourteen at the time. Celia and I had not seen each other since I had left Norway in 1951, so we had a lot of catching up to do.

It had been an amazing holiday, and I returned to Montreal in high spirits. The trip had been so stimulating that I felt as if I were walking on air for days. Getting back into my routine at work and home took a great deal of effort.

There is a saying that husbands and wives should never work together, and there were times when I felt this to be absolutely true. But from the beginning, I had decided that if Stefan and I were to have a reasonably good working relationship, he would be the boss and I his secretary. He was, after all, an excellent and prudent businessperson who made all the important business decisions, and, like any good secretary, I tried to keep order in the office and facilitate his work as much as I could.

In the fall of 1974, Helen entered Vanier College and Marvin continued taking courses at McGill University. Both of them had part-time jobs, Helen at Coles Bookstore and Marvin as a ski instructor at the International Ski School. Through the university, Marvin became aware of the plight of Soviet Jewry and participated in demonstrations and meetings concerning this issue. Despite the children's different schedules, we still managed to have supper together at 6:00 p.m. most days.

Stefan's and my twenty-fifth wedding anniversary was coming up in December of 1974, and, to celebrate this milestone, we went to Hawaii. It was a dream come true for me. We went on a tour that included Oahu, Kauai, Maui and Hawaii. Stefan was especially excited to visit Pearl Harbor. Coincidentally, our friends Judith and Victor Farkas were in Honolulu at the time, so we had dinner together. Even though it has been nearly thirty years since that outstanding trip, I can recall almost every detail.

One day soon after we returned from our trip to Hawaii, I came home to find Marvin in the den with a stranger. My first thought was, who is this girl and what is she doing here? The girl who was sitting comfortably in one of our leather armchairs could not have been more than sixteen years old to Marvin's twenty. Marvin introduced her as Lily and told me that he was helping her with some of her homework. She had transferred from a school in Rosemère to Montreal's Hebrew Academy for her last year of high school and was staying with her grandparents in Montreal during the week. The explanation seemed plausible at the time.

But Lily turned up at our home more and more often, and it soon became apparent that there was more to this relationship than tutor and student. Lily was a very attractive and self-assured young woman who seemed older than her years. She and Marvin had many common interests as she, too, was becoming religious — hence her transfer to Hebrew Academy. Their relationship quickly developed into a major romance, and it was not long before Lily called Stefan and me Ma and Pa, albeit jokingly. Stefan and I had our reservations about where this romance was headed. Surely, Marvin and Lily could not be thinking of getting married. They were much too young, and Marvin had not even completed his education. But I don't think Stefan or I ever voiced our concerns to Marvin.

While we were speculating, the two made plans. Lily had decided to spend the year after high school at a yeshiva for young women in Israel. I was relieved when I heard about her plans. A year's separation would be a cooling-off period for the young couple and would give them a chance to contemplate their relationship from a distance. However, that was not to be. Marvin declared that he could not be separated from Lily for such a long time, and so he made inquiries about an ORT engineering school in Tel Aviv and applied for admittance.

The school year at Vanier College ended in late April, and Helen went to Israel for the summer with a youth group, which included her boyfriend, Mark, and two of her girlfriends. I kept some of the letters she sent Stefan and me from the kibbutz where she spent the first few weeks and read them again recently. We must have been so happy when we received these letters. They are descriptive, funny and precious. Helen, who came to love the kibbutz and the people there, wished she could spend the rest of the summer working in the fields and swimming in the big pool. However, her group left the kibbutz at the beginning of July to tour Israel.

When Marvin and Lily left for Israel, our house became very empty. I had the distinct feeling that Marvin would never really live with us anymore. Helen, too, was away a great deal. I had given her my car to drive while I drove Marvin's brown Toyota, and she had now become completely independent. Her life was busy with school, work, riding her horse and, of course, Mark. She had a curfew of 1:00 a.m. on weekends, and she was hardly ever late. I used to fall asleep after Helen went out but woke up again and lay awake until I heard her come in. I was never at ease until she was safely at home.

Lily and Marvin were barely settled in their respective schools in Israel when they decided that neither of the schools was suitable for them. It was easy for Lily to switch to a program for foreign students at Bar Ilan University, but Marvin resolved that, rather than going to school, he would go back to Kibbutz Tirat Zvi as a volunteer. No amount of objection or cajoling on our part could persuade him to change his mind. Both Stefan and I feared that this would be the end of Marvin's formal education. How would Marvin be able to earn a living? We were upset and disappointed. This was not the way it was supposed to happen. We realized that our children were not ours any longer and had to lead their lives as they chose — a hard pill for us to swallow.

Lily enjoyed her course at Bar Ilan, while Marvin worked in the fields of Tirat Zvi. They spent most weekends together either in Tel Aviv or at the kibbutz. Both of them wrote to us regularly.

That winter, Stefan and I went to South America. We joined a tour that took us to Brazil, Argentina and Peru. The train ride to the station where we would board a bus to Machu Picchu was spectacular. I couldn't stop looking out the window at the scenery outside. Forests of tall trees lined the train tracks, and small rivers blinked in the sun. A bus took us up to the Incan ruins of Machu Picchu along winding and narrow roads, but the sight that greeted us was well worth the trip. It was breathtaking. This excursion to Machu Picchu was the highlight of the entire trip.

On our way home, we stopped in Miami, where Stefan declared that he had travelled enough and would not go on any more trips if he could help it. He wanted us to buy an apartment condo in Florida, where we would spend our winter vacations. We had often spoken about such a possibility. I could no longer really object; we had seen a lot of the world. In between the trips I have described, we also went on a trip to Asia that took us to Taiwan, Japan, Thailand, Hong Kong and Singapore, as well as trips to Bermuda, California, Freeport and Nassau, and several to Miami Beach.

The following day in Miami, we set out in our rental car on Interstate 95 in search of Palm Aire Golf and Country Club in Pompano

Beach, a development that had been recommended to us by friends. Palm Aire appeared to be a beautiful development, and we were soon the proud owners of Unit 108 at 2851 South Palm Aire Drive. For years to come, during the winter months, we would spend three weeks at Palm Aire and return home for six.

In the late winter of 1975, a letter arrived from Lily telling us that she and Marvin had decided to marry. They would return from Israel at the end of the school year and get married sometime in the summer. A separate letter from Marvin arrived shortly thereafter confirming this news. Both Stefan and I were shocked. Although we had been reasonably sure that Lily and Marvin were serious about their relationship, we had thought they would wait to get married until they were somewhat older.

In order to discuss the situation with Lily's parents, Simi and Peter, we invited them to our house one afternoon. If I had expected them to oppose their daughter's marriage at the age of not quite eighteen, I was in for a surprise. They talked blithely about the wedding, where and when it would take place, seemingly without worry about how the young couple would manage after the festivities were over. Stefan, however, had thought long and hard about this problem and come up with a solution. Lily and Marvin could move to London, Ontario, where Marvin could oversee, with Stefan's help, the development of a tract of land that Stefan had bought.

As Helen grew into adulthood, I became somewhat excessively attuned to her moods. When she was happy, so was I, and when she was unhappy, I suffered with her. Even when she moved away and her tone of voice on the telephone was sad, I got upset. Did I expect her to be eternally happy? I knew that could never be. It was only when she married that I let go, but still today, after living apart for so many years, I am sensitive to the tone of her voice.

Lily and Marvin returned to Montreal in the spring of 1976. We had of course told them about the land purchase in London, Ontario, and about the opportunity for Marvin to develop this project. It was a foregone conclusion that he would not continue his education at McGill University. He had enjoyed his work in Quebec City and was now looking forward to getting started in London.

It was a busy summer for all of us. Helen attended a French course at the Université de Montréal, Marvin and Stefan spent a lot of time in London to prepare for the construction of the project, and I participated in the wedding arrangements. Before we knew it, it was August, only one week away from the wedding on August 8. I had ordered beautiful flower arrangements for the tables, but, at the last minute, Lily and Marvin decided to forego the flowers and donate the money we would have spent on them to Israel. I thought this was a touching gesture and clearly so did the florist. When we entered the room for the wedding dinner, we saw that small bud vases with flowers adorned each table, which the florist had arranged at no cost to us.

Their wedding was one of the most lively and wonderful weddings I have ever attended. Lily, looking radiant, led everyone in Israeli dances, and her enthusiasm was so infectious that Marvin even persuaded my seventy-four-year-old mother to dance with him. Looking recently through the album of this wedding has made me very sad. One picture shows the beautiful bride with her attractive parents, her pretty younger sisters and her brother. In photos of our family, Stefan and I are beaming, and Helen, looking lovely in her long gown, is smiling. And there is Marvin, laughing with Greg, his best man. And, of course, there are pictures of the bride and groom. Where have the years gone?

And so Lily and Marvin were gone. It took some adjustment, but I knew we would see them often. Marvin had always been very close to us, and I had come to love Lily. I thought of her as a daughter rather than as a daughter-in-law.

The following year, Helen decided that the time had come to leave Montreal. Most likely she also felt that she had lived at home long enough, which, combined with the political situation — René Lévesque's Parti Québécois had come into power and many young people had left the province — convinced her to apply for admittance to the University of Toronto, where she was accepted. And when she went to Israel in the summer of 1977, I knew that Helen, too, had left home for good.

Alone Again

Ever since my mother came to Canada, I had felt responsible for her, but as she grew older, my feelings of responsibility increased. When my mother turned seventy-five in 1977, I realized that the time had come for her to move to a seniors' residence. She had been travelling less and less in the last few years and was quite lonely. Several of her friends had passed away, others were unwell and her bridge games had become few and far between. We visited the King David residence and rented a spacious one-bedroom apartment with a balcony. She would be farther away from us than she had ever been while in Montreal, since the King David was located in Côte St-Luc.

It was a difficult time for my mother. She had to get rid of many of her treasured belongings because they would not all fit into the new apartment. She chose her favourite things to keep, among them her desk and portable typewriter. My mother had learned to type when she was young, and her letters, like mine, were always typewritten.

My mother adjusted well to her new life at the King David. She felt safe there because there were always people around. I came to realize that she liked to be looked after, which made the situation much easier for me, then and later. How different I am from my mother! I treasure my independence and will not give in, although the time has now come for me to make some concessions, I struggle and fight, and at times I do not understand the point of it all. But I suppose that I am still my father's daughter, because that is exactly what he did until the end.

About a year after my mother moved to the seniors' residence, she was diagnosed with kidney cancer. At the time, it was not customary to tell patients more than what they wanted to know, and my mother was not curious. When I spoke to her doctor, he told me, much to my relief, that in her case no chemotherapy was indicated. She was subsequently hospitalized at St. Mary's Hospital a couple of times, but she never asked any questions.

On a balmy summer evening in June 1978, the phone rang. It was Marvin with the most unexpected news: Lily was pregnant. I don't know why I was as shocked as I was. My first thoughts were: I am not ready to be a grandmother yet, Lily is still studying, they are too young — it cannot be! But it was. Lily felt relatively well. She was continuing school and already making plans for what to do with the baby after it was born. One thing was sure: she would graduate as planned.

Our little grandson was born in London, Ontario, on March 11, 1979, and when I laid eyes on this sturdy, healthy little boy for the first time, I no longer doubted that I was ready to be a grandma. The baby was named Mordechai after my father and would be called Motti. When the baby was just a few days old, Marvin told us that, on the day Motti was born, he had promised Lily that they would make aliyah — move to Israel — in two to three years. When I heard this news, I felt a deep sense of loss, as though their departure were imminent. The joy I had felt at becoming a grandparent was instantly marred. We stayed in London until the *brit milah* was over and returned to Montreal filled with mixed emotions.

That spring, Helen graduated from the University of Toronto with a Bachelor of Science degree. She had been working part-time for a veterinarian, and soon after she graduated, she got her first full-time job with Pitman-Moore, a company that sold veterinary pharmaceuticals. She had been living in her own apartment for about a year, and for obvious reasons, we began to see less of her. She had a few friends, found opportunities to ride horses, and if she was lonely, she never said so. But I could not help worrying about her just the same.

In the spring of 1979, after spending a few weeks in Palm Beach, Florida, with her cousin Claire, my mother returned home and was hardly able to walk. I took her to a bone specialist who proclaimed that she was too old to spend much time on. This was the most shocking thing I had ever heard, and I got her out of the doctor's office as fast as I could. Her condition deteriorated, and before Pesach that year, I persuaded her to spend the two seder nights at our house, with the understanding that we would bring her to St. Mary's Hospital at the end of the holidays. Marvin and Lily came from London with the baby, Helen from Toronto, and we had two quiet seders with my mother. Stefan and I had given her our bedroom with its adjoining washroom, but I was constantly worried that she would fall. In the end, we realized that she had to be taken to the hospital by ambulance. My heart sank when I watched her leave my house on a stretcher.

Dr. Villemure, a neurosurgeon, who was called in from the Montreal Neurological Institute, convinced my mother and me that back surgery was indicated despite her age of seventy-seven. He assured me that if she were his mother, he would opt for such an operation, as otherwise she would be in a wheelchair for the rest of her life. And so it was that my mother's back was operated on at the Montreal Neurological Institute.

She spent the first night after the operation in the Intensive Care Unit, and when I called the hospital a few times that night to inquire about her condition, I was told that her breathing was laboured. Eventually I realized that her breathing problems might be due to her lifelong smoking habit, and the nurse I subsequently spoke to on the phone confirmed this. When I arrived the next day at the hospital, my mother was lying on her back in one of the small rooms adjacent to the nurses' station — smoking a cigarette! Although cigarette smoking was then allowed in hospitals in Quebec, I was shocked.

From the hospital, my mother was transferred to a convalescent home, where she had to learn how to walk again. Since she was an exceedingly optimistic person, she was convinced that she would recover. And walk she did, albeit with a cane and a great deal of difficulty. The King David could not take her back under the circumstances, as all its residents had to be totally self-sufficient. As always, my mother was very compliant. If moving to a nursing home was the solution, so be it. Once again she had to get rid of some of her furnishings, and this time only her beloved desk and typewriter followed her to the Villa Maria Nursing Home. There my mother was well looked after, and the nurses loved her. Because my mother was still reasonably ambulatory, she had few, if any, complaints.

I had always maintained that I would not leave our home on Vincent Street until we could find a condo we could buy, and in the fall of 1979 we found one that was being built in Côte St-Luc. The building would be located facing a park. We moved in April 1980, leaving the house that had been my anchor for twenty years, and I never looked back.

Our new condo unit was spacious and comfortable with almost as much room as our house. It consisted of an entrance hall that led to a cozy den on the left and a living room straight ahead. The dining room next to the living room was adjacent to the kitchen. My favourite room came next. This is the room that contained all my toys: a computer, a printer, a fax machine and a typewriter. A very large bedroom completed our new home. I had never found the stairs of our split-level bungalow an inconvenience, but having no stairs at all made life easier. I had thought that moving to a condominium was a sign of old age, but we have been here twenty-five years now.

Lily and Marvin also moved in 1980. A small bungalow had been put up for sale at a reasonable price, and Marvin considered the house a good buy. Lily graduated from the University of Western Ontario that summer, and we proudly watched her as she received her certificate, wearing the customary black hat and gown.

That same year, Helen, on a visit to Montreal, announced that she had a new boyfriend, Murray. She had known Murray, also an ex-Montrealer, for some time, and they had been just friends until recently when she realized that her feelings for him had deepened. She promised to bring Murray home to meet us and was sure that we would like him, too. Hearing that great news, I began to worry less about my daughter.

My mother was still reasonably well, and I visited her in the nursing home about three times a week. She was able to come to our place frequently, but of course not nearly as often as before. It was obvious that walking was difficult for her, and the symptoms of her kidney cancer caused her to be hospitalized from time to time. But she still never asked any questions. Although my mother was smart and may have suspected what was wrong with her, she did not want to talk about it. When Lily, Marvin and Motti came for visits to Montreal, she showed little interest in her great-grandchild. Perhaps it was just too much for her to be around such a young child.

In October that year, Helen and Murray came to Montreal, primarily to visit his sister, who had recently given birth to a little boy, her third. Both Stefan and I liked Murray immediately. What we saw was a slight young man, a few years older than Helen, well-spoken and intelligent. At the time, he was working for a small advertising agency, although his Honours BA was in Psychology. It was obvious to me that he and Helen had a special relationship, and I hoped that in time it would develop into something more. I did not have long to wait. In January 1981, they announced their engagement.

We met Murray's parents, Rose and Natan, and his sister Annie and brother-in-law Bernie. Rose and Natan were originally from Poland and Holocaust survivors. Natan had lost his first family in the camps, and Rose and he met immediately after the war and married. They had worked hard and now lived in the downstairs apartment of their own duplex while Annie and her family lived upstairs.

Helen and Murray did not want to have a long engagement and decided to get married in July 1981. The Beth Ora synagogue had a hall available for July 12, a Sunday. I began scurrying around to get things organized.

Lily and Marvin had in the meantime also formulated their plans. Marvin had done well in London, overseeing the building and rental of several commercial properties. He and Lily planned to go to Israel for six weeks the day after the wedding to make inquiries about apartments and job opportunities, and to make aliyah shortly thereafter. Lily had told me early in the spring that year that she wanted to become pregnant with their second child as soon as possible, and, at a wedding in Toronto in June, she confided in me that she was in fact pregnant again. Would this interfere with their plans? I asked. Of course not, was Lily's reply.

The big day arrived. The synagogue looked lovely, and so did the bride. I had known in advance that this wedding would differ from Lily and Marvin's simcha (celebration). Neither Murray nor Helen wanted a particularly Jewish affair with a lot of horas (traditional Jewish dance) and Hebrew music, but a wedding is always fun. There were new people to meet, mostly Murray's friends, and our own guests to entertain. Little Motti, an adorable two-year-old, kept everyone busy. My friend Sigmund had arrived a few days earlier and planned to stay on after the wedding. And the event we had been planning for months was over in a few short hours.

Two weeks later, the nursing home called to tell me that my mother had had to be taken to the hospital by ambulance and was now in the emergency department. Stefan was not at home, so I drove my car to St. Mary's. Again my mother stayed in the hospital a few days and was then transferred back to the Villa Maria Nursing Home, considerably weaker than before. She had no pain, she said, but it was obvious that my mother's life was waning.

Any hope I had that Lily and Marvin would ultimately find it too difficult to make aliyah was quickly dashed when they returned from Israel. They had been promised an apartment in an excellent area of Jerusalem, and with the money they would receive from the sale of their house and furnishings and Marvin's share of the sale of one of the buildings in London, they would be able to manage in the beginning. Fortunately, Lily was feeling well, and soon after they went back to London, they began preparing for their departure.

The company Helen worked for in 1981, Pitman-Moore, closed its doors that year. Since her office was located on the premises of Ortho Pharmaceutical, she noticed in a posting one day that a position in its Regulatory Affairs Department was open. She applied for and got the job. There Helen began to climb the corporate ladder, although no one could have foreseen just how successful she eventually would be. Murray, too, made a change. He left his job and together with a partner, David, started a small advertising agency called Ellis Teichman Communications Ltd. Although their combined incomes were modest, Helen and Murray managed well, with Murray taking care of their finances. They even talked about buying their first house in the near future.

Both Helen and Murray were working hard. Murray's advertising business made steady progress, and eventually he and his partner were able to move to larger and more fashionable premises. Helen had soon realized that promotions required special efforts, one of which was to become noticed. Her suggestion to start an exercise program for the employees at Ortho Pharmaceutical was well received, and for a while it was a successful undertaking. It achieved what Helen had intended: she became known not only for her hard work and her intelligent approach, but also because of her extra effort.

I was apprehensive that fall. Marvin and family's impending departure filled me with dread, and my mother's steadily declining health was worrying to say the least. Although she was in a good nursing home, I came to realize the importance of family being closely involved with a patient's care and of making daily inquiries about her condition. As usual, my work kept me on an even keel, and I was thankful for the diversion it gave me.

One major event followed another. Marvin, Lily and Motti came to stay with us for a few days before they left for Israel. We picked up my mother on October 27, the day before her seventy-ninth birthday and the day before Marvin and family were to leave. I can still see the scene in our hall when my mother, sitting in a wheelchair, said goodbye to her grandson and his family. She was very courageous, although she must have known that she would not see them again. I was on the verge of tears but did not dare to give vent to my feelings for fear I would upset everybody, including my mother.

A few days after Lily, Marvin and Motti left, I had a disturbing phone call from my mother. She had been moved upstairs to another floor (the nurses obviously felt she needed more care), and when she had had to go to the bathroom at night, she had fallen because she did not know her way in the dark. I was terribly upset. When I got to the nursing home, I found her in a somewhat confused state and re-quested that she be moved back to her old room immediately. At this point, I knew that my mother was seriously ill and would most likely not have long to live. Shortly afterwards, the nursing home called to say my mother had fallen again, she was confused and they had sent her to St. Mary's Hospital by ambulance.

When I arrived at the emergency room, my mother did not rec-ognize me and muttered something unintelligible. Later that evening, she was moved to a private room upstairs and given oxygen. A phone call from her doctor confirmed what I already knew. My mother was dying from kidney failure, but he felt that she would live through the night. Early next morning, Stefan and I went to the hospital. My mother was lying on her side, breathing heavily, unaware of us or her surroundings. I was a coward; I could not bear to watch her death struggle and sat in the waiting room with Stefan, knitting boo-ties for my new grandchild. One death, one birth. Once my mother had passed away, we went into the room. She was lying on her back, peaceful at last, and I was glad that her suffering had come to an end.

The discussions at Paperman and Sons funeral home about the type of casket in which to bury my mother were totally distressing, as was my conversation with the rabbi. I had never met this rabbi before because he was working at Beth Ora synagogue only temporarily. It took some persuasion on my part to get him to agree that I would write the obituary and he would read it in its entirety at the funeral service. How could he describe my mother, never having spoken to her? Since our family was small, even smaller with Lily, Marvin and Motti gone, and since we had not had time to have the obituary published prior to the funeral, the chapel at Paperman and Sons was more than large enough. Only a few people attended the service and fewer still came to the cemetery. When the service was over and I, being the only close relative, walked away from the grave on the narrow path made for me by those who were present, I felt very much alone and isolated.

When the shiva was over, I went back to work. It was strange not having to worry about my mother any more. She had been constantly on my mind during the past few years. As is common in these situations, I had become the mother and she the child, although only figuratively speaking. My mother was bright and alert almost until the very end, but, as her only child, I had been responsible for everything relating to her care. We had also become closer during those later years, and I had felt a great deal of pity for her. Now that she was gone forever, I felt empty.

But life goes on. I had my routine at work and home. We drove to Toronto quite frequently to visit Helen and Murray and enjoyed spending time with them. In the meantime, Lily and Marvin got settled in Jerusalem. Marvin tried his luck as a real estate agent, with little success, while Lily went to an *ulpan* to improve her Hebrew. As Lily had promised, she wrote to us often. Her warm, loving and descriptive letters, combined with frequent phone calls, made us feel connected. We were overjoyed when she gave birth on January 31, 1982, to a healthy little boy at the Hadassah hospital in Jerusalem.

We could not get on a flight in time for the *brit milah*. An ad in the *Canadian Jewish News* attracted our attention — a package deal including six nights at the King David Hotel in Jerusalem. Our travel agent made a reservation for us, and, without telling Lily and Marvin of our plans, we arrived in Jerusalem when little Shmuli was about nine days old. It was a wonderful surprise for Lily and Marvin.

This was the first of our many trips to visit Lily and Marvin in Israel. Each time I was so happy to see them, and we had such wonderful times with them. But my joy was always mixed with sadness because I knew our time together was only temporary and we would have to say goodbye again. Our visits to Israel upset my equilibrium, and it took me a few days to recover and get back to normal. I believe that few things are quite as difficult as living so far from your loved ones. And in those days, Israel was safe.

Each time we were in Israel, Marvin took a few days off work and drove us to various places in the country. Eventually, there was hardly a place that we had not visited. My cousins Erna and Erwin had in the meantime moved to Nahariya, a town in northern Israel. On a visit to this town, we found them in good health and very content. Erna loved the nearby sea, and Erwin spent his days at Regba Kitchens, a moshav (cooperative agricultural community) where he had the opportunity to work with wood — the kind of work he loved. As many German Jews lived in Nahariya, Erna and Erwin had made friends among them, and they often met for coffee in the afternoons. Both Erna and Erwin had adjusted remarkably well to life in Israel, and although their sons, David and Paul, both lived and worked in Jerusalem, they did not intend to make another move any time soon.

Marvin had given up the real estate business and had bought a document storage business, which was somewhat more profitable. But without our help, Lily and Marvin would have been unable to stay in Israel. This upset me sometimes. It was a paradox: I wanted nothing better than for them to come back to Canada, yet we kept on sending them money to enable them to stay in Israel. Then finally a promising opportunity presented itself. Two Canadian business-people approached Marvin. Would he be interested in building and developing a storage centre? Marvin quickly sold his document storage centre, and because he found a site for the new storage centre not far from Petah Tikva, that is where his family moved in 1983. It was a good move.

Since both our children were living out of town, I led a pretty quiet life. At the time, our travelling was limited to trips to Toronto and to Israel, and in the summer of 1984, we were once again on our way to visit our family in Petah Tikva. Lily was in the early stages of her third pregnancy and feeling rather unwell. However, being the good sport that she was, she never objected to the special trips Marvin had planned for all of us, and we once again made the most of the few weeks we had together.

When Stefan and I left Israel this time, we knew that we would see Marvin and his family again before long, so the parting was less difficult. Lily was anxious to come for a visit to Canada, primarily to see her aging grandfather (her grandmother had passed away after Lily moved to Israel). Travelling with two little boys would be difficult, but it would be even harder with a third child. So it was decided that Lily and the boys would come to Canada in October for six weeks, and Marvin would join them for the last two so that they could go home together.

Lily was radiant when she arrived. The trip had not been too difficult, she felt well and she was looking forward to her stay in Montreal. Motti, then five years old, and Shmoo (Shmuli), then two and a half, quickly adjusted to their new surroundings. Before we knew it, Marvin arrived from Israel, and he and his family were off to Toronto to visit old friends. When they all left six weeks later, it was with our promise that we would visit them in Israel after the birth of the new baby.

Joy and Sorrow

It turned out that we had two new grandchildren to look forward to in 1985. Helen told us in early December 1984 that she was pregnant. I was overjoyed, but since she was and still is a very tiny woman, and mostly because I am her mother, I was somewhat concerned lest her small size become a problem during her pregnancy.

When Helen and Murray joined us in Florida for a few days in the sun at the end of 1984, she was not feeling too well. Stefan and I celebrated our thirty-fifth wedding anniversary that year with a big party at our Florida home, but Helen was too unwell to participate, even though she made a valiant effort. I had hired a musician to make the evening more festive, and, by the look of things, I succeeded. It has always been my motto to mark the milestones in my life with a celebration in our home, and I felt that thirty-five years of married life was well worth such a celebration. Too bad that Helen had to spend the evening lying on Stefan's and my bed in the darkened bedroom!

Stefan and I went to Toronto in March 1985 for Murray's birthday. Helen was feeling well by then, and we enjoyed our visit to their new home in Thornhill. We drove back home on March 11, and late in the evening, when we were already half asleep, the phone rang. It was Marvin. Lily had given birth to a little girl, and they were overjoyed. They would call her Shoshana after my mother (my mother's second name was Johanna), which means "rose" in Hebrew. Mother and baby were doing fine.

I could hardly sleep, I was so excited. Even the following day I felt that I was walking on air. No one could wish for more. Two adorable grandsons followed by a little girl! I pictured how happy Lily and Marvin must be. But that evening another phone call came. Marvin sounded upset. He told us Lily was quite sick and asked if I could come to Israel. We could take the baby home while Lily remained in hospital. He thought she would have to stay there for a while.

Stefan and I were stunned. We quickly threw things into suitcases and were on the evening flight to Tel Aviv. I had called Helen and Murray to let them know what was happening. Helen was in the fourth month of her pregnancy, and I hated to upset her. But it could not be helped under the circumstances.

During the trip, I was extremely nervous, so much so that most of the time my body shook uncontrollably. I had the most horrible premonition; I could neither eat nor sleep. Stefan on the other hand was optimistic. Lily was healthy when the baby was born, and nothing that terrible could have happened during the last two days. He was sure that everything would be all right. But it was not. When the plane landed in Tel Aviv, our names were called. We were told to disembark ahead of the other passengers. Then we knew. One look at Marvin's face confirmed that the unthinkable had happened: Lily had died that morning. At that moment, my fear was mostly for Stefan. The shock was almost too much for him. He looked ghastly pale and all he could do was throw his arms about Marvin and cry with him. And so the three of us stood together in the crowded airport, crying and in a world of our own.

I cannot remember our ride to Petah Tikva. The sequence of events was so confusing at that moment that they were impossible to grasp. The baby, who was fine, was still in the hospital where she was born. We would have to pick her up after the funeral the next day. Neighbours were looking after Motti and Shmuli, but Motti came home in the afternoon, looking surprised to find us there. People brought in food, but none of us could eat in our exhaustion and despair. I called

Helen and heard her cry of disbelief and sorrow. I could not offer any consolation. She wanted to come, but Murray did not want her to, due to her pregnancy.

Someone put the boys to bed. Marvin told us to sleep in his and Lily's bedroom; he would not be able to sleep there anyhow. And then after a long and sleepless night, the morning of the funeral arrived. Marvin had decided that Motti, who was six years old, was still too young to attend, so Stefan, Marvin and I rode to the cemetery alone.

Every time I visit Lily's grave and see the chapel to which her body was brought on a gurney, I see before me the strands of her long beautiful hair that had escaped her shroud. I thought I was going to collapse with grief. It was my beloved daughter-in-law's funeral we were attending. How could such a thing happen? When her body was lowered into the ground and my son was standing in the tall grass around her grave, crying brokenly, I could only cry with him.

That afternoon, we went to the hospital to see our little granddaughter for the first time. It was love at first sight. In the middle of a horrendous tragedy, a beautiful innocent baby had been born, whose care and well-being would be the sole responsibility of her father. How would he be able to manage?

It would take years until I was finally able to look at pictures of Lily. When I went back to our Florida apartment in the winter of 1985, I immediately removed a beautiful picture that hung on my bedroom wall. The picture shows a happy, smiling family — Marvin, Lily and their two little boys. Lily, who was already pregnant with Shoshana, was positively radiant. Years later, I gave this picture to my granddaughter, and I hope that she treasures it as I did.

When Shoshana was brought home, a nurse had been hired to take care of her at night, so that we would all be able to sleep. During the day, we took care of her. I was very nervous. The responsibility for this tiny baby weighed heavily on me, even though Stefan and Marvin hardly ever left me alone with her. The boys were back in school and *gan* (daycare), respectively. I am fairly sure that not even

Motti understood the concept of death yet, and with Stefan and me living with them, which was unusual, they did not seem to miss *Ima* (Mommy). At least they did not say much about her absence.

Around Pesach, we decided that all of us should go back to Montreal. I was very relieved that I was going home. Perhaps things would fall into place once I was in my own surroundings. I knew that I would be able to handle our problems better in the comfort of my own place.

We gave our large bedroom to Marvin and the boys. The first night, they all slept in the same bed; then we arranged for a cot. Little Shoshana stayed in our second bedroom. My young neighbour Rhonda lent me all her baby equipment, including a crib, a changing table, a carriage and even a bunting bag because it was still cold outside. I appreciated her kindness. We hired a nurse to take care of Shoshana at night.

The seder night was difficult. We had ordered the food from a caterer, but I could barely look at it. Even now, I have an aversion to ordering food for Pesach. Somehow the next few weeks passed. We knew Marvin had to make a decision sooner or later — and we waited. In the end, he decided to go back to Israel. We persuaded him to leave the baby with us until he got settled and had arranged for help. When he left with the boys, we felt terrible.

Now that Shoshana was going to remain with us for a while, we hired a full-time nurse. The baby became the centre of our universe. When the nurse was off, we took turns taking care of Shoshana at night. And when she gave us her first toothless smile, we thought we had won the lottery. She was adorable. Her hair was becoming reddish, her complexion was white and whoever went into the nursery to see her was always rewarded with her smile. We bonded with her forever.

When Shoshana was four months old, Marvin decided that, as difficult as it might be for him, she had to come to Israel to join the family. Stefan and I knew that he was right, but we would have loved to keep her with us for just a little while longer.

We had decided that I would fly to Israel with the baby, stay in Petah Tikva for a few days and then make a detour to Norway on my way home. I needed something to look forward to after my departure from Israel.

A call to Helen brought more disturbing news. Her gynecologist had told her that he thought the fetus was too small. As much as I tried to console her by saying, "You have at least four more weeks left until you give birth; the baby grows a lot in those last weeks," my words sounded lame even to me. Now we could do nothing but wait. I was, if possible, even more on edge than before.

The last night I spent in Petah Tikva was very hot, so I decided to move my bedding to the floor of the porch. During the late evening, Motti came to me crying. He did not want me to leave. I felt awful. That night, we slept on the floor together.

Leaving the baby was so hard. I worried endlessly. When I looked in on her just before we left for the airport, I saw her in her favourite position in her crib: rocking on all fours with her little bum covered by only a diaper. That sight is etched in my memory. I was sad beyond description when I left Marvin and the boys at the airport. I did not know how he would manage with the added responsibility of a baby. But Marvin was wonderful. He smiled and told me not to worry and that we would be in touch. I promised that Stefan and I would visit again soon, and then I was on my own.

I arrived in Oslo in the evening, to find Beks waiting for me at the airport. This time, I stayed in Norway only a few days. I was anxious to get back home because of Helen's fast-approaching due date. When I called Helen, she was in a much better frame of mind. At her last checkup, her gynecologist had assured her that the fetus had had a growth spurt and that he was no longer worried about its size. As always, just walking the streets of Oslo and hearing the familiar language spoken all around me put the spring back into my step and made me feel more optimistic. The short side trip had served its purpose.

Stefan and I went to see Helen a few days before she was due to give birth. She was well and anxious to get the ordeal over with. Soon after we arrived home, there was a phone call from Murray informing us that Helen had delivered a baby girl weighing six pounds. Mother and child were fine. Instead of being relieved and happy that all was well, I suddenly became very nervous and anxious and could not wait to get back into the car to drive to Toronto. I had to see Helen and the baby with my own eyes to convince myself that they were both fine.

That evening, we went to see Helen and her little daughter. The baby was sleeping in a crib next to Helen's bed. She was so sweet — a tuft of black hair covered her head, and the little face was heart-shaped. She actually resembled her dad a bit when she was a newborn. She was to be called Erin, a name that was totally unfamiliar to me then.

We visited again when she was three months old, an adorable baby whose smile could melt stones. It was just before Helen was due to go back to work. She had hired a Swedish nanny to take care of Erin but was very reluctant to leave her. At that point, she would gladly have given up any thoughts of a career and stayed at home. But as hard as it was, she went back to work.

In October of 1985, just before we were leaving for Israel to visit Marvin and his children, Stefan felt a curious pain on the top of his head when he showered. When the pain travelled down to his eye, he went to see his doctor. Doctor Gomberg diagnosed his condition immediately but told Stefan only that it was a form of neuralgia. He gave him a prescription in case the pain got worse, and we left for Israel on schedule.

Motti and Shmuli were really happy to see us again. The baby was sleeping when we arrived, and I marvelled that she did not wake up in all the commotion. She had grown so much during the past few months! Her hair was still reddish and looked like it would become curly in time. When she woke up, she smiled at us as though she knew us. Obviously, she was used to strangers.

Marvin had rented an apartment for us near the beach in Herzliya, and Stefan and I walked on the beach every morning. It was beautiful and relaxing. Then we would buy some rolls for breakfast and wait to hear from Marvin. Most days he came to pick us up, despite the fact that he was quite busy. The storage centre had now become a reality, and although its construction was not yet finished, we were impressed with what he had accomplished during a time of such personal difficulties. Some of the storage cubicles had already been rented, and Marvin felt that this venture would turn out to be very successful.

One evening when we were watching the news on TV in Marvin's living room, Stefan suddenly moaned and held his head. This was his first severe pain with what turned out to be trigeminal neuralgia, more commonly known as tic douloureux. The three of us became very concerned, and the following morning Marvin took Stefan to a neurologist, who immediately recognized the symptoms. He advised Stefan to start taking the medication that Dr. Gomberg had prescribed and confirmed that it was a certain type of neuralgia that would probably go away again by itself.

After three weeks in Israel, we returned home. It was difficult to leave Marvin and the children. Although Marvin never complained, we knew that his life was filled with hardship and there was little Stefan and I could do to help.

The pain that Stefan had experienced in Israel was fortunately infrequent at first, but Stefan never felt really well. Less severe tics plagued him constantly, and the neurologist in Montreal, whom we consulted, increased his medication. The pills caused Stefan to be tired all the time, so he slept a lot and found it difficult to concentrate. The illness literally took over our lives. Stefan felt better intermittently, but the worry about further attacks was always with him — and me. When his pain was severe and he insisted that he could drive his car anyway, I was nervous and tense until he returned. I had to force myself to go on with my daily activities.

We tried to go to Toronto every six weeks or so to see little Erin. New toys, appropriate for her age, appeared between each of our visits, and we could see that this child would never lack for anything. Both Murray and Helen spent every free minute with the baby and took her along wherever they went on weekends. Their nanny took good care of Erin in their absence.

Stefan was planning to visit Marvin by himself in the winter of 1986. He had felt reasonably well for a while and was anxious to see Marvin and the children. A date for his departure had been set. To our surprise, Marvin asked him to postpone his trip for a little while. He had met a woman with whom he wanted to spend as much time as possible, since she was only a visitor to Israel. He had met Gail.

Global Connections

During the winter of 1986, Marvin's friends began urging him to start dating. He met with a few young women over coffee, none of whom acknowledged the existence of his three children. For Marvin, their omission immediately ended what had not even begun. Marvin eventually met Gail through his friends Mindy and Johnny, who had come from England years earlier and belonged to the Anglo-American Modern Orthodox group that had befriended Lily and Marvin.

Gail and Mindy were friends from England, and when Gail came to Israel to spend a few days with Mindy and Johnny, Marvin was invited to their home for a purpose. Gail was unattached, had never been married and had no children. She was twenty-six years old, a lawyer by profession and from a Modern Orthodox background. Mindy thought that perhaps Gail and Marvin might become interested in each other. And she was right.

Marvin and Gail went out a few times before Gail met his kids. She was very impressed with the three of them. They obviously behaved well in her presence, and no one could possibly resist little Shoshana's smile. When Gail went back to England, it was with the understanding that she and Marvin would continue seeing each other either in Israel or in Manchester. It was a brief courtship. Gail spent Pesach with Marvin and the children at a hotel in Israel, and Marvin went to England for a brief visit. When we spoke to him, he sounded happier than he had in a long time. And the announcement was not long in coming. He and Gail would get married — when and where had not been decided yet. What had been decided, though, was that they would live in Montreal for the next two years. Gail did not want to live in Petah Tikva, where everyone had known Lily, until she felt more secure in her role as a mother to Marvin's children.

This was a wonderful turn of events for us. We immediately began looking for a small house for Marvin's family and found a condominium townhouse not far from where we lived. Marvin and the children were due to arrive in Montreal in June, and Gail would arrive a week before in order to be here to welcome her future family. They would all stay with us until the repairs to their house had been completed.

I had spoken to Gail several times on the phone, so we were able to identify each other when I met her at the airport. A pleasant-looking young woman pulling a carry-on turned out to be my future daughter-in-law. After the first awkward minutes, we soon found common ground. Gail was an agreeable house guest. She was a cultured and knowledgeable person with whom it was easy to get along.

I showed her their house, and she was very happy with it — there would be enough room for everybody and some privacy for her and Marvin. In our conversations, we also touched upon the objections her parents had to her marriage plans. I told her that I could well understand them, but, when all was said and done, it was her life. I hoped she realized the difficulties she would invariably face.

Before we knew it, the day came for the rest of the family to arrive. I remember that Gail put some toys on the bed in our bedroom so that the children would have a nice surprise waiting for them. I was very touched by this gesture.

Stefan, Gail and I went to the airport to meet Marvin and the children. After a long wait, we saw them finally emerge, Shoshana in Marvin's arms and the boys running to meet us. When Shoshana saw Gail, she said "Gailie" and leaned toward her. I had a momentary pang of jealousy, but how could the baby possibly have recognized us? In the six months we had not seen her, she had turned into a beautiful little girl, with reddish wavy hair and the same sweet smile she had always had. Marvin called her Shooshoo, a name that has stuck to her even until today.

Gail and Marvin got married in Manchester, England, and unfortunately we could not attend the wedding, as we needed to take care of the children. When the two returned to Montreal as husband and wife, Marvin seemed much happier for a while. He had been well received by Gail's parents and relatives, and the wedding and reception had been lovely. The couple had spent one day in a luxury hotel before coming back to Canada. To celebrate the occasion, I hosted a party at our house, to which I invited all our friends.

~

Stefan's illness came in waves. There were times when he suffered terribly with his tics and took a lot of medication, and other times when the tics decreased and he managed with fewer pills. He was never totally at ease, so neither was I. In the summer of 1987, Stefan found the pain of his neuralgia almost unbearable. He took the maximum medication his body could tolerate and would fall asleep as soon as he sat down. Our neurologist finally consented to referring him to the then-chief of neurosurgery at the Jewish General Hospital for what they referred to as a "procedure." Because Stefan was in such agonizing pain most of the time, the hospital admitted him as soon as the request was made. What we did not know was that the chief of neurosurgery was away on holiday and wasn't due to return until two weeks later. In the meantime, Stefan became weaker and more demoralized with every day he spent in the hospital.

When the chief of neurosurgery finally returned from his vacation, he explained to us what he would do to eliminate or at least lessen the pain Stefan was enduring. With the help of a special machine, he would burn part of the trigeminal nerve. Since the procedure might endanger the proper functioning of Stefan's left eye (the side of his face that was affected), he would take care not to go too deep. Stefan would stay in hospital the day of the procedure but would be released the following day.

The first few days at home following the procedure were exceedingly difficult. Stefan was weak, in a great deal of pain and very discouraged. But as the days passed, his pain lessened, and for more than a year he managed with very little medication. Our lives became more normal again.

~

Gail came to Florida with Shooshoo in March 1988. I was very surprised when Gail told me that she was pregnant. The baby was due in August. Shooshoo was as cute as ever. During their visit, Stefan caught a cold and lost his voice, so all he could do was whisper. One day, when Shooshoo was sitting on his lap, she began whispering to him, perhaps thinking that this was the normal way for them to communicate. Then and many times in the ensuing years, there were moments when I loved this little girl so much that it hurt.

Two babies were expected in 1988 — Gail's in August and Helen's second child in November. I can recall a visit to Helen and her family that summer. They were already in their new, large home, and when Helen returned from Ottawa late in the afternoon, I thought, She really looks like a young executive. Dressed in a lovely summery maternity dress and carrying a briefcase, her appearance was that of the consummate businessperson she had already become. Her business travels were mostly confined to day trips then.

Gail worked in the office until just before Ashi was born. Gail's parents arrived in time for the *brit milah*, and so we finally met our in-laws. Both Stefan and I liked the Yaffes immediately. Gail's father was a doctor my age and about ten years older than her mother. Ashi was their first grandchild, and they were delighted.

The *brit milah* for our youngest grandson, Benjamin, was held at Helen and Murray's home. The services of an old friend of Marvin's from London, Ontario, who was both a *mohel* and a pediatrician, had been engaged, and the ceremony was quickly over.

In October that year, we moved into a new, bigger condo unit in Florida, which stood us in good stead that winter. Marvin, Gail and their children came down to Florida for the winter vacation, as did Gail's sister Estelle and a friend of hers, Johnny. While Estelle and Johnny did not stay with us, we saw a lot of them, and they were nice to have around. It was a very happy time for me. I loved showing off our new condo, where I was actually able to make room for Marvin's whole family. While they were with us, we celebrated my sixtieth birthday. I felt physically young and strong and fortunate to have our cute grandchildren around me. Marvin, Motti, Shmoo and Shooshoo loved the pool, and their squeals of joy could be heard from miles away.

For me personally, 1989 was a big year — it was the year of the computer. Stefan had enjoyed our new Florida condo so much that he made plans to spend much more time there in the winter. But what would I do with my work? I could not possibly stay away for weeks on end and still keep on working and I had no intention of giving it up. The solution was obvious: I had to become computer literate. Gail offered to be my tutor. We bought an NEC laptop computer, which did not look anything like the sleek laptops of today. After the software was installed, Gail gave me my first lesson — how to turn the computer on and off.

Frankly, I was totally scared of this new tool that I would have to master before the onset of the coming winter. We had bought the computer in June, and in order to practise, I decided to enter all the figures between January, the beginning of our fiscal year, and June. For two weeks, Gail was constantly available on the phone whenever I needed her and had even compiled a tutorial for me as added help. No one could have been more devoted to the cause than she was, and by the time Stefan and I went to Russia and Norway that summer, I had mastered both the bookkeeping program and WordPerfect. I was thrilled.

~

I had wanted to go back to Norway for a visit, and since Stefan was still feeling reasonably well and was not taking too much medication for his tic douloureux, we decided to take a tour in Russia and end our trip with three days in Norway. It was our first big trip in quite some time, and I was really looking forward to it. Russia was not a country that was visited by tourists a great deal at that time. We flew to Helsinki, Finland, stayed there for a day and then continued on to Moscow the following day. My first and lasting impression of Moscow was that the city was hot, big and old.

We stayed in Moscow for three days and were taken to the different tourist sites, among them the Kremlin and the nearby famous GUM department store. With its arcades and high ceilings, this store was like nothing we had ever seen before.

From Moscow, we flew to Kiev. The following day was Friday, and when we returned in the afternoon to our hotel from our sightseeing tour of the city, Stefan and I were astonished to see two Hasidic Jews in full regalia, long black coats and black hats, waiting for the elevator. Needless to say, they aroused our curiosity, so Stefan went over to speak to them. It turned out that they were teachers from New York who had come to Russia to bring prayer books and visit the few remaining Jews in the city.

They told us the location of the synagogue in Kiev and invited us to their room for kiddush (a blessing over wine that ushers in Shabbat) around 10:00 p.m. that evening. Shabbat would start very late because sundown in Kiev would be around that time. In the evening, we went to the synagogue. It was before Shabbat, but a few congregants had already arrived in the old and dark synagogue. A young man who spoke a bit of English told us that he was studying Hebrew in preparation for making aliyah to Israel.

From there, we went to Babi Yar on the outskirts of the city. The evening was cool and rainy, and the sight of the ravine, where so many Jews had lost their lives during the Holocaust, was unspeakably sad.

When we returned to the hotel, we decided to pay the two teachers from New York a visit. It turned out to be an unforgettable Erev Shabbat (eve of Shabbat). A candle had been lit on the small night table between the two cots in the room. The room, which was as tiny as ours, was incredibly neat. Our hosts had managed to stow away their suitcases underneath their cots and had created an atmosphere of total calm in preparation for Shabbat. We were each handed a paper cup with wine, and, instead of bread, they produced a slice of matzo. They explained that they had brought all their food with them for the duration of their two-week stay, since they had not known if there would be any kosher food available in Russia. So while prayer books occupied one of their suitcases, the other was filled with assorted foods, such as tuna, matzo and various other items that would not spoil. I could not help but admire their resolve, and I think the others felt the same way. This was an encounter none of us would ever forget.

Our next stop was Yalta, the beautiful resort city on the Black Sea, also famous because of the Yalta Conference that took place there at the end of World War II. Our hotel was located near the beach, which was crowded at this time of the year, mostly with Russian vacationers.

We flew to Leningrad (now Saint Petersburg) three days later and arrived there at 10:30 at night in brilliant sunshine. I had not experienced the midnight sun for a long time, and the scene was almost surreal. Leningrad is the most amazing city, beautiful beyond belief with its bridges, palaces and the famous Hermitage. A hovercraft took us to Catherine the Great's summer palace, where we spent hours visiting its ornate rooms and gardens, and the following day, we spent a few hours at the Hermitage.

The following day we left for Oslo, where we spent three wonderful days. We walked the familiar streets, visited with Beks and her sister Hanna and bought trolls and *lusekofter* (hand-knitted Norwegian sweaters) for the children. I promised myself that my next visit would be much longer.

In November that year, we left for Florida for a four-month stay. What I remember of that winter 1989–1990 was that we lived day to day. On good days, when Stefan felt well, we were happy, and on bad days, we hoped that the next day would be better.

The following winter, Stefan finally underwent a second procedure for his tic douloureux, this time at the Montreal Neurological Institute. Dr. Prokrupa was more concerned about eliminating Stefan's pain than preserving the function of his left eye when performing the radio-frequency procedure, and the outcome was a complete success. From the moment I saw Stefan in his room at the hospital following the procedure, I knew he was no longer in pain. Even today we are still grateful for Dr. Prokrupa's intervention.

In the spring of 1991, many members of the Meieran family came to Montreal on their way to Ottawa, where they were to attend Renée's daughter Linn's graduation. I had spent a day with Linn in Montreal during the preceding winter and found her to be a lovely young woman. She was majoring in journalism and had big plans, as most young people do. Now that she had accomplished the first step on her journey, her family had come to wish her well. Beks stayed with us, Renée and Erik at Ruby Foo's Hotel. Linn's father, her younger half-brother and her other grandmother had gone straight to Ottawa.

Helen, Murray and their children came to Montreal to meet Beks, Renée and Erik, and on that Sunday morning, all the grandchildren and their parents came to our place for brunch. What fun we had! I had bought the kids presents in honour of this get-together. Our visitors, including Beks, who was seventy-nine years old at the time, spoke English. I was so happy that day, having my old friends meet my family at long last. Stefan and I promised to attend Beks's eightieth birthday in Oslo the following year.

Motti's bar mitzvah took place in March 1992, and we celebrated Stefan's seventieth birthday in June 1992. Stefan's birthday signalled the beginning of his retirement.

In November that year, Marvin and Gail separated. I felt terribly sorry for Marvin and the children, who suffered tremendously under the strain. Ashi was only four years old and very attached to his *abba* (father) and his siblings, especially to Shooshoo. The boys had gotten used to their new mother and loved her. Gail was the only mother Shooshoo knew. Ashi was to live with Gail and spend every other weekend at Marvin's house. Visiting rights had been drawn up for the other children. Many difficult and painful situations arose in the aftermath of the separation, which naturally affected all our lives.

The Medal

Marvin had often urged me to get in touch with Yad Vashem in Jerusalem to apply for a medal for Einar Wellén, who had risked his life to rescue my parents and me during the war. For one reason or another, I had never acted on it, but I realized one day that the years were going by and we were not getting any younger. I wrote my first letter to Yad Vashem on June 1, 1994, and then waited. Months went by, and finally, in September of 1994, a letter arrived from Yad Vashem. The Yad Vashem staff asked me to supply information about Einar's life, as well as my own, during the many years since the war. Had he saved other Jewish lives? How old was he in 1943? My story would have to be notarized either by a rabbi or a notary. I did not waste a day; that same evening I sat down at my computer and rewrote the story in accordance with the requested format. I made an appointment with the rabbi at the Beth Ora synagogue, who signed my application. The rabbi informed me that it would take at least a year for Yad Vashem to process my request. Why was I so apprehensive?

In February 1995, I received a letter from Yad Vashem acknowledging receipt of my testimony. My file had now been placed on the agenda of the Commission for the Designation of the Righteous. The letter urged patience, since many files were waiting to be examined. By May, nearly one year since I had first contacted Yad Vashem, there was still no news. Yet another inquiry was sent back to me with a brief notation from Dr. M. Paldiel, who was then the Director of the Department of the Righteous, indicating that my file was currently on the agenda of the commission and that I would be advised shortly of its decision.

I went to Norway that summer, June 1995. It was a wonderful trip, which included revisiting Buahaugen for the first time since I had been there with my parents during the war. However, I found Einar Wellén in poor health, and Yad Vashem had not yet granted my request for a medal for him. He was suffering from unexplained pains, and it was evident that he had become somewhat forgetful. It was also apparent that he was taking a great deal of medication to relieve his pain, which could explain his memory lapses. Yet his family blamed his condition on nerves; I had very serious doubts. It was while visiting Buahaugen that I told Marit, Einar's wife and my dear friend, that I had applied to Yad Vashem for a medal for Einar, but that I did not yet know what the outcome would be.

After this trip to Norway, in August 1995, I once again wrote to Yad Vashem expressing my concern about Einar Wellén's deteriorating health and my fear that he might be suffering from Alzheimer's and would soon be unable to attend a ceremony in his honour. Fortunately, my diagnosis was wrong, but he became seriously ill that fall and was near death. Einar was seventy-one years old when I wrote my first letter to Yad Vashem. Despite the fact that I had been under the impression that he was in good health, I was concerned and impatient from the very first day I mailed my letter to Jerusalem.

I received no reply, and by October I was becoming frantic. During my frequent phone calls to Einar and Marit, Einar always sounded well and happy to hear from me. His pain was said to be due to a healing rib fracture from a fall while skiing. I was doubtful but said nothing of course. My old friend Celia, who lives in Jerusalem, contacted Yad Vashem and was told that my file would come before the commission in November. Yet another letter to Dr. Paldiel produced no clarification.

An opportunity presented itself in the person of Josi Kersen. Josi is my grandchildren's aunt and was Lily's youngest sister. She made aliyah with the rest of her family when she was twelve years old, went to school in Israel and subsequently served in the Israeli army. After being discharged, she came back to North America, living and working in New York for a number of years. Now she was on her way back to Israel, this time to remain. She came to Montreal for the High Holidays in the fall of 1995, and before she left, I asked her to look into the situation at Yad Vashem. As a Hebrew-speaking person, she should be able to get accurate information.

And that she did. Only a few days after Josi arrived in Israel, a fax came with the news that the commission had approved my request on October 29. I felt so exhilarated, as though I had received a most wonderful gift. My whole family shared my excitement as we waited for the written confirmation from Yad Vashem.

Stefan and I were to leave for Florida on November 12 to spend the winter months there. I had spoken to Einar and Marit about three weeks earlier and had planned to call them from Florida as soon as we were settled.

The Saturday before we were scheduled to leave, I found a message on my answering machine from Marit. My heart sank. She had never called me before, and I feared the worst. Marit's calm voice answered the phone. She thanked me for my last letter — I was holding my breath — and then she quietly told me that Einar had had two serious operations on his stomach, one day after another, on Monday and Tuesday. On Tuesday, they had, in fact, almost lost him. He was now in critical condition, drifting in and out of consciousness. They would not know for ten days whether cancer was the reason for the large bleeding ulcer that had been found. I was devastated.

For the next three or four weeks, the news was bad. Einar did not seem to improve. He was still sleeping most of the day and when he was awake he did not make much sense. I kept in touch as best I could, by phone and then by fax. I will always be grateful to Nina,

Einar and Marit's daughter, for keeping me informed almost every second day.

And then, finally, Einar's condition improved. One of Marit's concerns, now that he was recovering, was to provide him with as much stimulation as possible. With this in mind, she suggested that a letter from me might serve this purpose. To my great surprise and joy, shortly after I wrote to Einar, I received a handwritten letter from him by fax. I could hardly believe my eyes. There was no question that, by some miracle, Einar was recovering. The biopsy that had been taken during the surgery was negative, and his prognosis was now excellent.

His family, particularly Marit, Nina and her husband, Knut, gathered around him to entice him to eat, and Knut, always selfless, spent much time walking the halls and staircases of the hospital with Einar to strengthen his wasted muscles. On Friday, December 8, Einar returned home, albeit weak and thin. Even his doctors marvelled at the speed of his recovery, which they attributed to the excellent physical condition Einar had been in prior to his illness.

On December 11, 1995, I received the long-awaited letter from Yad Vashem. Einar would receive a medal, a certificate and the title of "Righteous Among the Nations" for having been instrumental in saving my life during the war. The same day, Marvin, my son, faxed me a letter he had written to Einar to congratulate him and to explain to him the meaning of the honour he was to receive. The thought behind the letter and the letter itself moved me to tears. And if that were not enough for one day, later that afternoon Einar called to say hello. He, too, had received the letter from Yad Vashem. I realized immediately that he did not fully understand the meaning of this honour. He sounded weak and tired at the end of our conversation. Instead of trying to explain the matter to him on the phone, I wrote him another letter that day. As well, the United States Holocaust Memorial Museum in Washington sent him a letter of congratulations, upon my request. The letter was beautifully worded and could not leave any doubt as to the significance of the distinction he would be awarded.

At that point, I had no intentions of returning to Norway for the recognition ceremony, which I presumed would be a small affair arranged by the Israeli Embassy in Oslo. But on the morning following my conversation with Einar, Stefan made a startling announcement: "This is a major event," he said. "Not only are you going to the ceremony, but so will I." And once I thought about it, I knew that he was right. Marvin suggested that Yom Hashoah (Holocaust Remembrance Day) on April 16, 1996, would be a most appropriate day for such a ceremony; I should get in touch with the Israeli ambassador in Norway and ask his opinion in this matter. That same evening, I faxed a letter to Ambassador Michael Shiloh. The following morning, lo and behold, a reply arrived from Oslo. The ambassador concurred: Yom Hashoah would be a suitable day on which to hold this ceremony, hopefully in conjunction with the Jewish community in Oslo. The friendly tone of this letter added to my growing excitement.

A few days later, Marvin had big news: he would travel with us to Norway. He had always shown a great deal of interest in my background. His decision to visit Norway with us seemed only right.

Marvin was so intrigued with the events that, unbeknownst to me, he contacted the *Canadian Jewish News*. Would they be interested in this story? To my great surprise, I had a call one day from David Lazarus, a journalist at the paper. He had many questions. I explained to him that all the information he would require was contained in a speech I had already written for the ceremony. Details about my background in Germany could be found in the first part of my autobiography, which I also promised to fax him. I did not hear from him again and had no idea whether the newspaper would consider my story newsworthy. Stefan and I went home from Florida to Montreal in January 1996 for a few days. At that time, I contacted David Lazarus, who told me that the article about me would be in the paper either that week or the following one.

I was in the office when Stefan called to tell me that the article was in the paper. Motti had already heard about it from a schoolmate, and he had immediately called Stefan. I came home late that day and had barely finished reading the article when the phone rang. Someone I did not know, by the name of Cohen, was on the line. He had seen the article and was very interested. Could I explain more about where this had taken place and the circumstances of the rescue? I realized soon the reason for his special interest. His daughter, Libby, was living in Bergen, Norway, and was in Montreal visiting her parents. A long conversation between Libby and me followed. She promised to keep in touch with the Jewish community in Oslo to find out when the ceremony would take place, and if possible she would attend.

At the end of January, Stefan and I returned to Florida, where I found two phone messages from Ambassador Shiloh. When I returned his call, I spoke to his secretary, Chanan Goder, who was my contact at the Israeli Embassy in Norway. He immediately impressed me as being a kind and gentle person. He suggested I call Ken Harris, a member of the *Mosaiske Trossamfund* (Jewish community), who would be in charge of the Yom Hashoah arrangements and would be able to give me further details regarding the ceremony.

Ken Harris, an English Jew married to a Norwegian woman, began to outline for me his format for the recognition ceremony, which would include only two speakers — the Israeli Ambassador and the honouree. The ceremony was going to take place in the community centre, and there would be no reception after the ceremony. I suggested that I would like to have the opportunity to also say a few words, which resulted in a long back-and-forth discussion before he agreed to let me speak. The ceremony was also moved to the synagogue and grew to include a video presentation.

There was another matter to deal with. In my conversations with Einar, I understood that the thought of the ceremony and the limelight in which he would find himself made him quite nervous. I realized that he was not himself yet. It would take weeks and perhaps months for him to recover fully from his ordeal. One day I asked him whether he had told his friend Arne Myhrvold about the honour. It was Arne who had accompanied Einar on the rescue mission in 1943, and, until now, I had totally forgotten about him. Only about four years earlier, Einar had told me about Arne's participation, having assumed until then that I remembered him. Now Einar was embarrassed to tell Arne about the distinction he would be awarded. Since they are close friends, Einar did not want to keep this matter a secret, but how to tell Arne became a problem that weighed heavily on him.

Realizing and fully understanding Einar's dilemma, I became upset. I, too, felt that Arne was, and still is, deserving of a medal. The thought that I had inadvertently caused Einar such anguish upset me more than I can say. When Einar's letter arrived with the news that he had finally told Arne about the honour, I was as relieved as he was. He was now finally looking forward to the event, which, in a way, he had dreaded before. He mentioned again in this letter that he did not feel deserving of such an honour, but since the commission at Yad Vashem had found him worthy of this distinction, he was grateful and filled with pride for their consideration. His letter then went on to describe his life during the war, how he, too, had had to escape to Sweden and subsequently returned to Norway to carry out clandestine work for the Underground. He mentioned that this was the first time he had ever written about these events and that it was our friendship that had prompted him to finally do so. His letter restored my equilibrium.

My friend Renée Meieran had in the meantime translated my speech into Norwegian. It conveyed everything I wanted to say and lost nothing in its sensitive translation. I now began reading the Norwegian text out loud. I knew that the more I read it, the less chance there would be that my emotions would get the better of me during the ceremony.

It was during that time that I invited my daughter, Helen, to join us in Norway. Since she travelled extensively on business, I think I knew her answer in advance: an additional trip to Europe would be too much for her. Her decision was my loss and I believe hers as well.

A fax arrived from Ken Harris with the program for Yom Hashoah. I had promised him that we would sponsor a kiddush (small festive meal) on the following Shabbat, although I would be the only one of my family present (Stefan and Marvin would be in Budapest). Mr. Harris mentioned that he wanted me to speak again at the kiddush, since there would be younger and different people there than at the ceremony, and he wanted me to tell them who I was and why I was there.

During this, our last overseas telephone conversation, Mr. Harris mentioned that the Jewish community had heard of a man who was said to have been a driver in the Underground during the war. He had ostensibly transported Jews and Norwegians who had to escape to Sweden, from a barn on the outskirts of Oslo to a place within walking distance of the Swedish border. No one had known this man's name, and the driver had not known the names of any of those he had rescued on his truck. As he was a shy and modest man, he was certainly not looking for a medal, but the Jewish community was anxious to identify him. My speech, of which he had read a copy, had led Ken Harris to believe that I might have been on his truck. I told him that I would try to get in touch with this man during my stay in Norway.

A few days later, Stefan and I closed our condo in Florida and went home to Montreal. We celebrated Pesach together with our family, and two days after the conclusion of the holiday, Stefan, Marvin and I were on our way to Norway. I was excited and nervous. Motti had left with an event called the March of the Living the previous day.

We arrived in Amsterdam early in the morning on a bright and sunny day. The plane to Norway was delayed, and by the time we arrived in Oslo, I was totally exhausted, not having slept at all on the plane. There to meet us were Einar and Knut. Einar looked much thinner than when I had last seen him, but much healthier. Knut was, as always, smiling and helpful. The two drove us to our hotel. Next time we would meet would be at the synagogue the following evening.

I immediately contacted Ambassador Shiloh. He apologized that he could not meet with me prior to the ceremony the following day because he was busy with an Israeli delegation. My next phone call was to Ken Harris, who confirmed that everything was ready for the event, which would begin at 7:30 in the evening. Could we be there for about 7:15? A phone call to Beks followed. We would see her the same evening at her daughter Renée's home for dinner.

Renée's house, "Borgen" (the castle), is located in the suburban hills of Oslo. Two baby carriages were parked outside, so we knew that her young grandsons were there to welcome us. Beks looked wonderful despite her advancing years and the fact that she had been ill several times during the past few months. Renée's daughters, Lena and Linn, each had a little boy, who were introduced with great pride. Lena's son, Leo, was one and a half years old, with blond hair, brown eyes and apple-red cheeks. Liam, Linn's five-month-old, was olive-skinned with black hair and the most beautiful black eyes.

Renée had prepared a sumptuous meal. When Leo became a bit restless, Erik entertained him. He obviously enjoyed his role as *beste*, Leo's abbreviation for *bestefar* (grandfather). Although Stefan, Marvin and I were tired, we enjoyed the evening a lot. Old friends had come together and the conversation, mostly in English, flowed easily.

The following afternoon, Stefan, Marvin and I took the T-banen (the Oslo subway) to Sognsvann. This is a lake in the suburbs of Oslo. On the weekends, thousands of Norwegians take to the trails leading into the woods, hiking during the summer months and skiing during the winter.

Sognsvann is but one of several places where such trails begin. I love the stillness of the Norwegian woods, and it reminded me of years gone by. Now the lake was still frozen, and there was melting snow on the ground. Not far from there is the house where Stefan and I lived together for the first one and a half years of our married life. We walked down to Sognsveien 135 and showed Marvin where it all began.

By 6:30 p.m., we were ready to go to the synagogue. A police car was parked on the street, which reminded me, to my regret, that in Norway, too, there is still antisemitism. As added security, members of the Jewish community patrol the area around the synagogue within its gate. Ken Harris came out to greet us. He led us into the small synagogue, and apart from some children, we were the first to arrive. One of the children, a twelve-year-old girl, spoke to us in perfect English. She was Norwegian, she said, but went to English school. Three non-Jewish women were standing in the hall outside the sanctuary. When I asked them whether they were guests of the Wellén family, they answered, "No, we just came to watch." Soon a young man came forward and introduced himself as Chanan Goder. I had imagined him to be much older, but he was as kind and as pleasant as he had been on the telephone. Ambassador Shiloh, a distinguished-looking, tall, grey-haired diplomat, arrived soon after, accompanied by his wife.

Slowly, the narrow wooden benches of the old synagogue began to fill. Einar and Marit Wellén arrived with their immediate and extended family, as well as some close friends. Beks, Renée and Erik were there, too, and so was Lena. Josef Schattan, the cousin of a friend of ours in Montreal, whom we had met at his house a few years ago, came to say hello. And so did Herman and Ester Kahan, who somehow knew who we were, although we had not seen them since we left Norway. At exactly 7:30 p.m., the ceremony began and the hum of many voices died down.

Six candles were lit by survivors, Ambassador Shiloh and a young boy, whose candle represented the children who had perished in the Holocaust. The cantor chanted the prayer for the dead — "El Male Rachamim." The first speaker of the evening was Ambassador Shiloh. He spoke emotionally about the Holocaust — of the children who had died and deprived us of a generation of Jewish lives, of the antisemitism that remains rampant today even in Norway, and of the few who acted to save innocent lives during the war. At the conclusion of his speech, the ambassador presented the medal and the certificate of

Righteous Among the Nations to Einar Wellén. No doubt the memory of that moment will be treasured by all those who were present. I, for one, felt only gratitude that this long overdue recognition had come to pass.

Then it was my turn to speak. I did not dare look up from my paper. Since I had read the Norwegian text out loud many times, I managed to get through it almost without stumbling. I knew that I had the attention of the audience. It was quiet except for my own voice. When I returned to my seat, I saw that Marit was visibly moved. And so was Einar. He was the last speaker. He searched for his glasses, found them, put them on, only to take them off again. He began by thanking Yad Vashem for the honour. Then he spoke of his relationship with my father. I had not realized that Einar had had many conversations with my father, and his speech revealed how fond he had been of him and how much he had looked up to him. He also mentioned his friend Arne Myhrvold. About halfway through his speech, he put away the written text and wandered a bit from his prepared script. Everyone listened with great interest as he spoke of his clandestine work during the war.

The synagogue's choir, consisting of children and a few adults, sang several Hebrew songs suitable for the occasion. The president of the Oslo Jewish community then gave a brief speech. At the conclusion of the ceremony, Ken Harris read a poem written by a Norwegian Jew, now deceased, who had been a survivor of the Auschwitz concentration camp.

Several people came forward to greet me. Since I had introduced myself as Margrit Stenge, also known as Margrit Rosenberg, I was recognized by a few. But I had to ask their names. All but one person had changed too much for me to recognize them. Once I heard their names, though, I could see their young faces in my mind's eye. A paintbrush appeared to have added years to their features, and it took me a moment to get used to the transformation. Several people promised to attend the kiddush on Shabbat, which would give us more time to reminisce. Herman and Ester Kahan wanted Stefan,

Marvin and me to spend an evening with them. Only I could accept because Stefan and Marvin were leaving in two days.

Marit had prepared a reception in her and Einar's home for the guests. The champagne was flowing by the time we arrived (somewhat later than the others, having waited until the conclusion of the brief evening services), and the guests were helping themselves to wonderful open-faced sandwiches. We met many people we did not know, among them the former mayor of Oslo, Albert Nordengen, who was a close friend of Einar's. He had been a most beloved mayor for sixteen years. Also, we had the opportunity to view the medal in its small olive-wood box, as well as the accompanying certificate. I translated for Einar the greetings from Motti and Shmuli on a card that I had given to him during the ceremony, as well as the text of the inscription in the book that I had presented to him.

The following morning, Einar and Knut picked us up at our hotel, and soon we were on our way toward Valdres. It was a lovely, bright and even warm day, but almost as soon as we had left the city limits, remnants of snow were visible on the roadside. The lakes were still frozen, and as we drove through the beautiful Norwegian countryside, it was obvious that winter had not yet lost its grip. In fact, Easter is the most popular time to ski in Norway. The sun, when it shines, warms the air, and there is still a lot of snow in the mountains. And this was only two weeks after Easter, which had been early this year.

As we approached Rogne in the Valdres region, Knut wanted to know whether I would like him to drive to Volbu, where my school had been located, to give Stefan and Marvin an idea of how far the school had been from where my family had lived. I decided against it to spare Knut this detour. However, I pointed in the general direction across the lake, and I think they got a good idea of the distance I had had to walk or ski in order to reach my school. And then we climbed the road up to Buahaugen. This was the "new" road, not the one I had skied on each weekend in the spring of 1942. That road was closed until the summer months. Knut's van made the ascent to the top easily. The narrow road was surprisingly dry for this time of the year, and even when we reached the snowy landscape of Buahaugen, Knut expertly managed to reach the Wellén cabins.

Since I had been here the previous summer, Knut and Nina had added their own cottage, so now there were three cottages on the land that once was owned by Einar's uncle, Harald. Sitting on the bench outside the main cottage, warmed by the spring sun and with the melting snow beneath my feet, I looked at the snowy landscape all around me. This is what it had been like in the spring of 1942 when my parents had lived here in total isolation from the latter part of March until the end of June, when the farmers finally arrived for the summer. How could they have stood the loneliness, the lack of human contact, in addition to the daily struggle just to exist? There was still no electricity or running water in the area. My parents could not even fetch water from the small river nearby without skis. And when finally the spring sun thawed the snow and turned everything to mud, it became, if possible, even more difficult for them to carry out their daily chores. Just as during the war, all the cottages in the area were closed up, and only the sound of our voices disturbed the solitude of this mountain village.

Marvin asked me the following day whether my parents had appreciated that I made the difficult trip to Buahaugen by myself every weekend. My answer was a definite no. Had I met their expectations, I would have stayed with them at Buahaugen the whole time. And I knew this all too well even then.

During our descent from Buahaugen, Einar, Knut and I spoke of the last time we had been here, in June the previous year, when we had been looking for the Granlis' house. Since Einar had been in considerable pain at the time, we had given up our search, although we knew the general location of the house. Einar, too, had met Nils Granli at one time. It had now been twenty-two years since my summer trip to Norway when I had visited Alma Granli, living in the green house on the hill together with her daughter and her family.

Back in Rogne, Knut made inquiries because we simply could not find the house. Someone pointed us in the right direction, but we still could not identify the place we were looking for. Then Einar had a good idea. He would ask Mr. Skattebo, a carpenter from whom the family had bought some furniture. He would know everyone in the area. We stopped at his workshop. I remained in the van. Mr. Skattebo was outside, and Einar and Knut spoke to him. Suddenly Stefan came up to the van and excitedly said, "This man knew your parents." When Einar had asked him where the Granlis' house stood, he had pointed to a white house a short distance away and then said, "This is where the Granlis used to live, and during the war, a family by the name of Rosenberg lived there, too." I had goosebumps as I went to greet Mr. Skattebo. What had moved this man to mention my parents without being prompted? We spoke about old times for a while and then went inside to see his workshop. Mr. Skattebo was a fine carpenter, and Knut picked up a few smaller pieces of furniture, for resale in Oslo.

The Granlis' house was nearby, but I didn't recognize it. The white house before us looked like it had swallowed the little green house I knew. A young woman was outside watching four young kids playing in the mud and the melting snow. I explained to her that I had lived in this house for two years with the Granlis during the war. Yes, she said, she was familiar with the name, as she and her husband had bought the house from their daughter. They had modernized the house, so I would not have recognized it even if we had been able to go inside. However, since the woman had to watch the children, she could not invite us in. My story fascinated her, for she had never heard it before. We took some photos and then began our return trip to Oslo. The drive took about four and a half hours.

Stefan made an interesting observation. He believed my relationships with my Norwegian friends were different than the friendships I had formed in Canada. And perhaps he was right. All I know is that I am completely at ease when I am expressing myself in Norwegian.

Perhaps it is my feeling of contentment and my pleasure at still being able to converse fluently in Norwegian that influence my dialogue with my old and trusted friends.

The following day, Stefan and Marvin left for Budapest, and I moved to Beks's apartment. That afternoon, I phoned Ken Harris to ask for the name and telephone number of the member of the Norwegian Underground — the driver — of whom he had spoken during our last overseas telephone conversation. Mr. Harris told me that his name was Torleif Halvorsen. I dialled the number he gave me, and a cheerful woman's voice answered the phone. When I asked for Mr. Halvorsen, she said that he was unavailable at the moment; she was his wife, Kirsten. Would I tell her what it was about? When I did, she simply could not believe that someone would call after all these years. How had I heard about Torleif? Would I come to see them? I could get to Askim either by train or by bus, and the trip would take about one hour each way. I promised to look into schedules and to call her back the following day.

Marit and her twin sister, Lita, were celebrating their seventieth birthdays that evening. The party was called for 7:00. Marit, champagne glass in hand, greeted everyone at the downstairs entrance, looking a bit apprehensive at the gathering crowd. But then Einar welcomed us all and directed us toward a table plan, where we would find our names. Two large tables had been set up in an L-shape in Nina and Knut's first-floor apartment. All the furniture had been removed from their living-dining room to accommodate the large table. I was seated between Einar and his son Jan. Marit and her sister were sitting underneath a picture that had been painted when the twins were about four years old. It had been moved from Einar and Marit's upstairs apartment for the occasion, and I thought the idea was precious. Very soon I noticed the clever table plan. All the young people, Marit's and Lita's children and grandchildren, were placed between the older guests, enabling young and old to take pleasure in one another's company.

And then the party began. The many speeches were funny and were interspersed with songs written by friends and family. Dinner was served by the young members of the family, with none other than Knut in charge. I had the most wonderful time. Not for one minute did I feel like the outsider I was.

Early on in the evening, Einar said to me, "Margrit, you are the best *veninne* (female friend) I ever had." I was deeply moved. The wine was flowing, and by the time we got up from the table at 11:30, I may have been the only sober person at the party. Regrettably, I had to leave then, since I had to get up fairly early the following morning to attend Shabbat services and our kiddush. But the party lasted until 4:30 in the morning. From what I heard, all the guests that evening agreed that they had never attended a more wonderful affair.

The kiddush took place in the community centre adjoining the synagogue. A large table was laden with home-baked cakes and fruit, and small tables had been placed around the crowded room. One of the members of the congregation gave a brief explanation of the Torah reading that day, and I read the short speech I had prepared for the occasion. Then there was time for socializing with people I had known years ago and others who I just met. Among others, a young boy came to say hello and complimented me on my two speeches. It was nice to know that I had reached someone that young.

An old acquaintance, Leif Grusd, told me of an interesting project that he was participating in. Based on conversations with people who had fled by various means from Norway to Sweden during the war, project organizers had established the route most frequently used to reach the border. Children from the community were taken on excursions to see the distance their grandparents had had to walk to reach the safety of Sweden. Leif also mentioned that an official at that particular spot along the border had marked down all the names of the refugees passing through that point. He promised to look for the name Rosenberg the next time he was in the area, since I was not at all sure of where my family and I had crossed the border.

I was going to spend that evening with Ester and Herman Kahan. I had not known the couple well when I lived in Oslo after the war. Ester is a year or two younger than I, and Herman arrived in Norway in 1949. But I did remember them.

Herman picked me up in his large, well-appointed American car, and we drove to the suburbs of Oslo. One of his daughters and her Israeli husband greeted me in the entrance hall. They were on their way out, so it was just Herman, Ester and I who spent the evening together. We had many mutual acquaintances. Old photos were displayed, two of which showed the couple as I remembered them.

Herman's success story is remarkable. In 1949, on his way to America, he came to Norway to visit a sister who had settled there after the war. He liked what he saw and decided to remain there instead of going to the United States. He immediately started manufacturing stockings with a knitting machine he had brought from Hungary. Raw materials were still in extremely short supply, but he ripped up old stockings, from which new ones were produced. He worked day and night. He also realized that it was imperative to speak Norwegian well, and today he has only a very slight foreign accent. He understood early on that it was crucial for his growing business that he attend business school. And that, too, he did, in addition to keeping long hours at his factory. Ester helped out as much as she could in between giving birth to their children.

During the evening, we saw a video of Herman's seventieth birthday, an extravaganza that had taken place in one of the large hotels in the mountains. More than one hundred guests attended. All of them were treated to a sleigh ride, a lavish dinner that lasted half the night and brunch the following morning. In the video, I recognized several people I used to know.

Herman gave me a book based on his life that was written by a Norwegian writer. I put it aside, thinking that it would be just another story. Was I ever surprised when I began reading it back in Montreal. It is one of the most moving accounts of the war years I have ever read, written in a wonderful, simple style.

The next morning, I went to meet Torleif Halvorsen. The train to Askim left the railway station in downtown Oslo at 10:20 a.m. on Sunday morning. I had spoken to Kirsten Halvorsen the day before and told her which train I would be on. To identify myself, I said, "I am short and dark and will be wearing a raincoat regardless of the weather." She told me that she, too, was short and that we would have no problem spotting each other on the platform because few people would be getting off the train there.

As soon as the train left the city limits, the scenery changed dramatically. Forests, lakes and waterfalls were in abundance. This was also farm country. The small railway stations we stopped at were mostly private dwellings. Askim has recently been proclaimed a town, and its station is now larger. Kirsten had been right. We recognized each other immediately. She was taller and younger than I, with a pleasant face and a wonderful smile. With tears in her eyes, she hugged me like a long-lost friend and then immediately went on to say that Torleif was ill with a lung disease, that he did not hear well, that his memory was impaired and that he was extremely nervous — all this in the span of two minutes it took us to reach their van.

Torleif stepped down from the car, and I was happy that Kirsten had forewarned me. A small, shrunken old man, his clothes hanging loosely from his thin frame, came toward me. He shook my hand with downcast eyes and then returned to the driver's seat. The van was spacious and clean. The three of us had to sit in the front because there were no seats in the back of the van. Kirsten explained that they wanted to take me for a drive to the very barn where Torleif had picked up refugees during the war for the drive to the Swedish border. I was surprised that the barn was located in this area but was told that we were, in fact, getting closer to Oslo with each kilometre. As we drove farther away from Askim, the scenery changed. There were fewer and fewer farms, and we finally arrived at the barn. I had no memory of this place at all. My parents and I had been taken to a barn outside of Oslo during the night. It could very well have been this one, but I will never know.

We then continued toward the Swedish border. It was obvious that this area had been suited for Underground operations. No one lived there, but it was beautiful country. Dense forests of pine trees surrounded the many lakes of the region. The fog hung low over the mountains. As we drove along, Torleif appeared to be less nervous and spoke to me off and on. I told him what I remembered of the truck that had brought us to the border and of the trip itself. There were two things that came up in the conversation that jarred my memory. I recalled that, once everyone was on the truck, a tarpaulin had been stretched across the back to cover us. But still we had not left for quite a while. That, explained Torleif, was because hay was loaded on top of the tarpaulin, to give the truck the appearance of a hay wagon. Moreover, he mentioned a Swedish border town by the name of Charlottenberg. He would drive his truck to within half an hour's walk from the border and then follow his charges at a distance, to make sure that they were safe. Neither Kirsten nor Torleif doubted for one moment that I had been on one of his transports.

We were almost at the Swedish border when we turned back. Torleif was coughing constantly and was very cold. Since his hearing was poor, Kirsten told me some of his story. In February 1943, after having saved countless people whose names he never knew and who never knew his name, Torleif himself had had to leave Norway for the safety of Sweden. He was a young man with little education and was sent to northern Sweden to work, cutting lumber. There he met and married a woman and had two children with her. The marriage did not last, however. All his working life, Torleif drove trucks, and driving was the love of his life. He transported materials for road building, which was thought to have destroyed his lungs. I believe he was suffering from lung cancer or emphysema.

By this time, I am sure the whole village had heard about my arrival. In short order, Kirsten's son, Björn, and grandson arrived and then her daughter, whose name I cannot recall. Björn expressed his gratitude that finally someone who had been saved by Torleif had come to see him. I did not mention that I was not sure if I had been on one of his transports.

During our first telephone conversation, Kirsten inquired how I had heard about her husband, and had I told her about Ken Harris. What I did not know until later on was that it was Björn who had contacted the Swedish Jewish community, whose president he knew, about his stepfather's role during the war. The matter had been referred to the Jewish community in Oslo, and efforts had been made in vain to find someone who could identify Torleif Halvorsen, so that he could be recognized by Yad Vashem as Righteous Among the Nations. I realized then that he would never be a candidate for this honour. Sadly, the man was dying. But even if he had been well, the strain of such a ceremony would have been too much for him. I considered my visit to Askim a mitzvah (a good deed). I never indicated that I had been on his truck, but my presence in their house was gratifying to them, and I am sure that neither they nor I will ever forget our meeting.

My visit to Norway was quickly coming to an end. Monday evening, Nina, Knut, Einar, Marit and I went out to dinner together. We talked about the events of the past week, and I was sad that the trip was all over. So much had happened, and each of us would have his or her special memories of the recent days.

The following evening, it was time to say goodbye to Renée and Erik. Beks, Erik and I had dinner together at the Holmenkollen Restaurant, Beks's favourite. A brief visit to "Borgen," where Renée and Lena were waiting for us, and all that remained was just one more night in Oslo. Beks had been feeling unwell all day, and by the time I had to leave the next morning, she did not even let me embrace her for fear that I would catch her cold. It was Knut who drove me to the airport this time. All I could say to him was a simple thank you.

On the way back to Montreal, I thought to myself, what will I do now? The last five months had been filled with incredible excitement, and it was inevitable that I should feel a certain sadness and sense of loss. But I was comforted by the fact that the medal was resting in its little olive-wood box in Einar's house as testimony to the courage of a man who saved one life and thus a whole world.[3]

~

This particular trip to Norway catapulted me into an entirely new career. As I mentioned, Herman Kahan, a long-time acquaintance, had given me his biography on the evening I visited him and his wife, Ester. I was reluctant to read this book, since I had not read anything in Norwegian for many years, but once back in Montreal, I decided to take the plunge and was pleasantly surprised. Not only was it easy for me to read the language that I spoke fluently, but I loved the contents of the book so much that I decided to translate it into English so that my grandchildren would be able to read about Herman's remarkable journey through life.

I have since translated three other memoirs and two books by the Norwegian gentile writer Kristian Ottosen, one about the Norwegian Jews and one about Ravensbrück concentration camp.

---

3 As the Talmud states, "Whoever saves a life, it is considered as if he saved an entire world."

Old Friends and New

On March 11, 1997, Shooshoo turned twelve, so it was her bat mitzvah year. Because we were returning from Florida just a few days prior to her big day, I baked and froze all the cakes for the brunch, which I had planned in advance to celebrate the occasion, and packed them in their frozen state in my carry-on luggage for the trip home. When passing security, the ice-cold contents of my bags caused suspicion and then smiles when I told them what the contents were.

Shooshoo's bat mitzvah was observed in four stages: at Marvin's shul (synagogue), at the above-mentioned brunch, at a class b'not mitzvah (plural of "bat mitzvah") at the Beth David synagogue (more commonly known as the Baily shul) and then at a dinner at Beth David that night. Many of the b'not mitzvah girls looked very grown up in their long, fancy gowns and makeup. Shooshoo, who wore a suit I had bought for her in Florida, looked like the little girl she was. But for religious purposes, our little Shooshoo was now considered a woman.

On the night of the first seder that year, Allegra, her daughter, Corinne, and her nephew David came into our lives. Marvin and Allegra had met at the "Y." Allegra had been born in Egypt and had gone to Israel with her parents and two sisters when she was two years old. Life had been hard. Subsequently, the family immigrated to Canada and settled in Montreal.

The year 1997 turned out to be a big year for Helen, too. Throughout her years at Johnson & Johnson, she had received countless promotions and awards. She frequently travelled overseas and often gave presentations in countries in Europe, as well as in the United States. She was eventually promoted to director at her company in Toronto, and that spring she was offered a one-year position at Janssen Pharmaceuticals, the organization's company in Belgium, which she accepted.

In 1998, just before Rosh Hashanah, we visited Helen and her family in Belgium. It was a very memorable five-day vacation. The house Helen and Murray had rented was located on the outskirts of Antwerp in the little Flemish town of Kapellen, five kilometres from the Dutch border town of Putte. An iron gate led into the property, which looked like an estate with an expanse of beautifully tended green lawn surrounding it. The house, which had once been a Belgian duke's hunting lodge, was quite old but in very good condition.

Even the weather cooperated in the next few days. We visited Antwerp, where I spotted a beautiful necklace in the window of a jeweller in the diamond district, and decided that this would be my present for my upcoming seventieth birthday. As usual, there was no objection from my ever-generous husband, and I have worn this necklace ever since. On Rosh Hashanah, we attended services in a small synagogue in the morning and then drove to Brussels.

In Brussels, we visited Manneken Pis, the well-known sculpture and fountain, which I remembered from my stay in Brussels so many years ago, and we had lunch at an outdoor restaurant. On a different day, we visited Bruges, a beautiful medieval city with its waterways, where we could not resist a boat ride.

One day, Helen asked if we wanted to go to Knokke on the seashore. Knokke was in Belgium? When I was a young child, my parents used to take me to Knokke. In fact, I still have pictures of the three of us on the beach, but all these years I had been under the impression that Knokke was in France. I was thrilled to have the chance to revisit this place. So Helen, Stefan and I, plus their dog, Murphy, went to Knokke. Nothing about the place was familiar to me; after all, I had been there in what seemed like a different life. Still it felt strange to know that I had been on this very beach with my parents.

Another day, Murray drove us to an old Jewish cemetery, which was actually located in Holland. No one there pays much attention to the borders between Holland and Belgium. On our last day, before we left Amsterdam, we visited the house where Anne Frank and her parents had lived in hiding during the war. Having read so much about their ordeal, I found this visit very moving.

Since it takes only one and a half hours to fly from Amsterdam to Oslo, I decided to go on a three-day visit to Norway, whereas Stefan would fly straight to Montreal. Before the trip, I suggested to my eighty-six-year-old friend Beks that I would stay with Marit Wellén this time in order to spare Beks the trouble of having an extra person staying with her. She readily agreed.

For the last year, Marit had been living in her big apartment all by herself. Her husband, Einar, my rescuer and dear friend, had suffered a major stroke in 1997 and was now living in a nursing home. However, during the summer of 1998, Marit, her daughter, Nina, and Nina's husband, Knut, had brought Einar to their country house in Nevlunghavn by the sea. From their house, Einar was able to watch all the water activities, such as the regattas and speedboats. Even though he was unable to express his pleasure at being with his family, they knew that he loved being there, and for them this was their greatest joy. With the aid of two young helpers who came from the nearby town, Nina, Knut and Marit managed to care for Einar, who was helpless in his motorized wheelchair. Their effort was almost superhuman, but being who they were, they never thought about it that way. Marit and Einar's fiftieth wedding anniversary was celebrated with a big family party, with their three children and their grandchildren present.

Knut and Nina came to pick me up at the airport and drove me straight to their home in the suburbs of Oslo. I inquired about Einar and was told that he was as well as could be expected and that there had been no real change in his condition for about a year. As always, Marit and I were happy to spend time in each other's company, and we decided that we would visit Einar the following morning. I told Beks that I would see her that afternoon and that it was important that I visit Einar before anything else. I dreaded seeing my old friend in his deteriorated condition and prepared myself for a shock.

And, indeed, it was a shock. Nina wheeled him into the living room of the nursing home, as he could not handle his motorized wheelchair. There he was, a shadow of his former self, dressed in sweatpants and running shoes, his head bent. When Marit said, "Dear, here is Margrit," he looked up in surprise and said, "You still look like a young girl. How is Stefan?" I began to cry; it was heartbreaking. Nina and Marit were surprised that he still recognized me and knew my connection to Stefan. After a while, we took Einar back to his room, where Marit fed him his lunch and then one of my Belgian chocolates for dessert. A nurse came in to put him to bed for his nap. He was obviously happy when he saw her and forgot all about us. Marit kissed him goodbye and told him she would see him later, and then we left.

Voices woke me up in the middle of the night. I got up. The house was lit up, and Marit was standing in her small foyer ready to go out. She had just been called by the nursing home to inform her that Einar had become ill and had had to be taken to the hospital. He had, in fact, suffered another devastating stroke. I stayed in Oslo another two days and then had to leave. At the time, nothing mattered other than Einar's condition, which worsened daily. The outcome was inevitable. The day after I left, he died. Not knowing the customs observed by Norwegians when there is a death in the family, I asked Renée's husband, Erik, what would be the appropriate thing to do. He advised me to submit an obituary to *Aftenposten*, the Oslo daily newspaper, and to send flowers to Marit. That done, I felt a bit better. Once again, fate had been on my side. I had gone to Oslo just in time to see Einar once more, and he had lived long enough to know that the young girl whose life he had saved had never forgotten him.

I spent time with Beks, too, and, among other things, we discussed her situation. She was still living by herself in her apartment, but it had occurred to her that this was no longer safe, since she had fallen a few times. A move to the Oslo Jewish home for the elderly was an option, which she considered with some reluctance. I urged her to at least fill out an application form, as we knew that it would take a while before an apartment became available. Her heart was not in it, and it would take some time until she finally gave in and sent in the appropriate form. She was eighty-eight years old when she left the home she had lived in since the late 1930s. The day before I returned to Montreal, I had lunch with Beks and her granddaughter Lena. When I said goodbye to her at Majorstua, which was the bus and tram stop closest to her home, albeit still a good fifteen minutes' walk away, I watched her slight figure walk briskly away and wondered whether I would ever see her again.

Retirement

In December 1998, I turned seventy. Stefan and I celebrated with Marvin, Allegra and our grandchildren, Motti, Shmoo, Shooshoo and Ashi. Looking at pictures from the party, I see a lot of smiling faces. My grandchildren were the source of great pride to me then, as they had always been and still are. Despite the tragedy of Lily's loss and the many changes that followed, our family was tight-knit and seemingly indestructible.

Stefan and I next celebrated our fiftieth wedding anniversary, somewhat early, in October 1999. Helen, Marvin and Allegra looked after everything. I had always pictured a couple celebrating their golden anniversary as stout and sitting on a park bench, doing little else. But none of the people — all our contemporaries — who joined us at the Adath Israel synagogue in the suburb of Hampstead looked anything like my imaginary couple, including us, I believe. Many Montreal friends attended; others came from Toronto, Judith and Victor from Florida and my cousin Elfriede and her husband, Erik, from New York. This was the last time we saw Erik; he died a few years later of cancer.

Shooshoo and Erin performed a brief skit, which was a big success. The skit was followed by a few speeches, with Stefan being the last speaker. As always, he ad libbed and was very witty. I had jokingly told him that I thought I deserved a gold watch after so many years of service (in the office), so when he handed me a jewellery box at the end of his speech, I was sure that it contained this watch. To my astonishment, it was a gorgeous diamond bracelet, which almost took my breath away. Each time I wear it, it reminds me of a lovely party when our whole family was together, with the exception of Shmoo, who had already left to begin his studies at a yeshiva in Israel.

My friend Celia had told me the previous year that both she and I would be eligible for a certain amount of money that Norway paid its Jewish citizens as retribution for pain and suffering during the war, provided that they were at least sixteen years old at the end of the war. When I was in Norway in 1998, I mentioned to Marit's daughter and son-in-law that I did not feel that I was entitled to apply for this money as Norwegians had literally saved my life. Knut was adamant: it would be ridiculous of me not to accept what was being offered, and furthermore I should apply to the Norwegian government for a pension. He convinced me, I filled in applications for both and in no time, and without any further questions, I received $35,000 in retribution. As for the pension, when I was advised of its amount, another questionnaire was included for my husband in the event that he, too, had lived in Norway during World War II. And so it is that both Stefan and I receive small amounts each month from Norway. Strangely enough, Stefan receives twice as much as I do. I guess he deserves it more.

Stefan had promised Shmoo when he was still in Montreal that we would visit him in Israel that winter. I never made such a promise because I was not at all sure that I wanted to revisit the place that reminded me of so much sorrow. But I gave in and planned our trip, which would take us to Tel Aviv, Jerusalem and Eilat, as well as Petra in Jordan. We visited Shmoo at his yeshiva in Gush Etzion, and we all had dinner together with my cousins David and Ruth and my friend Celia. We then visited remarkable sites in Petra, spent two wonderful days in Eilat and saw Shmoo again in Jerusalem when he joined us for Shabbat.

Back in Montreal, I had finally retired from the work I had done for the last forty years. My son-in-law, Murray, took over my position. That winter was the first time in years that I was not working, although I continued doing translations. What seemed remarkable to me was that I did not miss my work then or even in the spring when we came home from Florida. I had genuinely enjoyed being part of the business for so many years, but once I turned over my work to Murray, I never looked back. I suppose that was just part of aging.

Over the years, Stefan and I proudly celebrated all of our children's and grandchildren's milestones and achievements. Helen became vice-president of a Washington-based pharmaceutical company, and eventually she and Murray established their own company. Marvin and Allegra got married, and Marvin took over the management of all of our properties. Motti graduated from McGill, made aliyah and married a lovely woman named Sara — they had a son, our first great-grandson, Yehuda Tzvi, who was born in 2005. Ashi and Ben both became a bar mitzvah. Shmoo attended a yeshiva in Israel. Shooshoo graduated from Hebrew Academy and then from Dawson College and eventually made aliyah. Erin and Ben both graduated from high school; Erin also graduated from university and Ben from community college. Allegra's daughter, Corinne, married a wonderful man named Yechiya.

∿

In the spring of 2002, our family attended a breakfast at the Beth Ora synagogue to commemorate the Holocaust. The speaker, Karin Doerr, was a petite woman, dressed in a long black dress. I was sitting too far off to one side to hear her speech in its entirety, but what I heard was of great interest to me. She was the co-writer of a Nazi-German–English lexicon that had recently been published, and I knew immediately that this was exactly what I had been looking for in the past two years. Kristian Ottosen, whose books I was translating at the time, used many German expressions for which I had not been able to find satisfactory counterparts in English. After the breakfast, I approached Karin Doerr and asked where I could buy this dictionary. Her reply was that it had not yet reached the university bookstores but that she would be glad to get a copy for me. We would meet as soon as a copy became available.

And so it was that I made a new and most unlikely friend. Karin, who is not Jewish, was born in Germany. She obtained her PhD in Montreal and, now in her fifties, teaches German language and a course called "Feminist Perspectives on Genocide" at Concordia University. Besides being a professor, she works tirelessly to spread the infamous history of the Holocaust, and has befriended many survivors in the course of her research. Strangely enough, we seem to have a common bond — the German language and books we read in our childhood. When we meet for lunch, we always have a great deal to talk about.

A website called "Women and the Holocaust" was established in 2001 by Judy Cohen, a Hungarian Holocaust survivor, and is used for educational purposes. During one of our meetings, Karin asked me if I could write down three short episodes from the war years that were especially memorable, to be posted on this website. That did not take me long, but even though Karin liked the stories, she said that they should be more explicit. Karin made suggestions and asked questions, and when my short memoirs were eventually published on the website, Judy Cohen asked if I could write my entire story, which I did some time later. It has now been published on "Women and the Holocaust," under "testimonies," as well as on a website called "Memoirs of Holocaust Survivors in Canada," which is under the auspices of professors Kyle Matthews and Frank Chalk of the Montreal Institute for Genocide and Human Rights Studies at Concordia University. I also wrote a review of the Nazi-German–English lexicon, which is also published on "Women and the Holocaust" under "reviews."

At a brunch that year at Karin's house, she briefly introduced me to a Holocaust survivor named Olga Sher, among other people. The following year, she mentioned to me that Olga had not felt comfortable telling her story to Steven Spielberg's foundation (USC Shoah Foundation, The Institute for Visual History and Education) and that she would prefer that someone write it for her. I became that someone. (I had written several such stories in the past years for friends Anne, Cila and Sigmund.)

Olga and I spent hours at my computer during the summer of 2003 and the winter of 2004 in Florida. By the time the story was finished, we had become friends. Olga was born and grew up in Poland. By some miracle, her whole family, consisting of her parents and her sister, managed to stay together in Poland throughout the war. Hers is a fascinating story of survival. The family left Poland after the war, lived in France for a few years and came to Canada in the late 1940s. Olga soon married a Canadian-born young man, Ben, with whom she could barely converse, since English was still a new language for her. Olga and Ben have two sons and a daughter. Both sons are professional writers. When her children had reached school age, Olga went back to university and obtained her Master of Arts degree. Subsequently, she became a teacher at the Jewish General Hospital, where her students were mostly children with emotional problems. She always kept busy with various activities, mainly relating to the Montreal Holocaust Museum. Olga's story is also published online through Concordia's "Memoirs of Holocaust Survivors in Canada."

For several months, I had been thinking of my long-time friend Beks's upcoming ninetieth birthday in October 2002. Should I go to Norway again? Stefan was very encouraging, and when Beks asked me during a telephone conversation a month before her big day where I was going to stay when in Oslo for her birthday, I knew what I had to do. And so it was that I spent six incredible days in Norway. However, I seriously doubt that I will ever go back again. Beks died in December that year. Beks's daughter Renée has taken over where her mother left off, corresponding with me through email, and I am happy that she, too, feels that there is a special bond between our two families.

In early December 2004, I received an email from an unknown source, Richard Oestermann, with the subject line "translation." He had obtained my email address from Celia in Jerusalem, who had recommended me highly as an accomplished translator (she has actually never read anything that I have translated). Richard explained briefly that he was an Israeli journalist, born in Denmark, who wrote articles for the Norwegian newspaper *Norge IDAG*. The editor of this paper had liked his articles about Israel so much that he had decided to publish a collection of these articles. The book would come out in Norway before Christmas. Someone in the United States had offered to finance the translation of the book from Norwegian into English, as well as the subsequent publication by an Israeli publishing house. He asked whether I would be interested in doing the translation, and, if so, he would send me a few pages of the book in Norwegian so that I could mail him a sample of my translation.

This was very exciting. But I wanted to be honest and told Richard that I had never translated anything professionally and therefore never had had a deadline. His reply was that, in this instance, I would be well paid in exchange for a three-month deadline and that the book, including many pictures, would consist of only about two hundred pages. I sent Richard the sample of my translation he requested, and he emailed to say he liked my work. A few weeks later, Richard advised me that I would be the translator of his book and that he could now tell me that I had competed with others. I was thrilled.

I received the Norwegian manuscript in January and devoted almost all the time I had to this project. I finished the translation in less than three months. I still have the copy of the cheque for $3,000, which I, at the age of seventy-six, received for my first professional translation job, and also, I thought at the time, my last. It is now September 2005 and the book has still not been published, but I understand that it will be published soon.[4]

---

4 Richard Oestermann's *Every Second Counts: True Stories from Israel* was published in 2006 by Gefen Books, with the English translation by Margrit Rosenberg Stenge.

So much has been written in these pages about the people in my life, but so little about Stefan, the person who has been at the centre of my world for so many years. It is now almost fifty-six years that we have been together, and today it is impossible for either of us to imagine life without the other. Now more than ever before, the phrase "until death do us part" has become a dreaded reality in our lives, and we are grateful for each day we spend together.

Stefan has been and still is the most generous of husbands, who wants only the best for me, his children and his grandchildren. Our grandchildren respect and love him, and I know they recognize that he is a special kind of grandpa, of which there are few. He is incredible for his age, eighty-three. He reads the newspaper from cover to cover, enjoys good books and music, and looks years younger than he is. His posture is still straight, he still plays golf — in short, he leads a very active life. He dresses extremely well, is slim and trim and is the best-looking elderly man I know.

I, on the other hand, am feeling my age. My movements are slow, I get easily tired and I miss the energy I once had. My waistline disappeared years ago, and I am often unhappy with my image in the mirror. I have few friends and have definitely become somewhat of a loner in the last few years. My computer plays a major role in my life, whether it is for writing, translating, playing bridge or seeking information on the internet.

And this is where I will end my story. True, I have had my share of regrets and disappointments, but overall my life has been rich and satisfying, and in many respects a life that people only dream about. Stefan and I have been blessed with good health, and, because of his foresightedness, we have been able to live extremely well. And even though I am sad that so few of our loved ones have remained near us, I do have wonderful memories of the times when we were all together, which will serve me well in the months or years to come.

Montreal, October 7, 2005

Epilogue: Stolpersteine and a Growing Family

Around 2010, a German-born friend told me about the Stolpersteine project. Stolpersteine (stumbling stones) were being installed in front of homes that had been owned in the past by Jews and others who were victims of the Nazis. I was not particularly interested in this project at the time and didn't investigate the significance of these stones.

At the end of 2015, our son, Marvin, happened to watch a TV program showing a journalist reporting on the installation of a Stolperstein in front of his childhood home. Stolpersteine are cobblestone-sized concrete cubes covered with brass plates, which are fitted into the existing sidewalks in front of such houses in Germany and in former Nazi-occupied countries. Each stone is recognizable by its inscription that always begins with the German words *Hier wohnte* (here lived) and includes the name and birth year of the individual, the year the person was either deported or escaped, and the countries of the individual's deportation or escape. This project is the largest memorial in the world and was initiated by the German artist Gunter Demnig in 1992.

Marvin has always been interested in my past, and he decided that the house on Marienburger Strasse 52 should be recognized as having been my parents' property and my childhood home. He searched the internet for contact information and got in touch with an individual named Ibrahim who was in charge of this project for the city of Cologne. It did not take long for Ibrahim to find out that my father, Markus Rosenberg, had in fact owned the house at Marienburger Strasse 52 and that we had lived there until 1938. He also quickly found all pertinent data, including my parents' birth years and my mother's maiden name. Both my husband and Marvin decided that a third stone should bear my name as well.

It occurred to me that two more stones should be added, one in the name of my aunt (my father's sister), Karolienchen Plaut, and one in her husband's name, Natan Plaut. This suddenly became very important to me. My aunt and uncle had remained in our house after my parents and I left quite suddenly in 1938, and following the death of my grandmother in Cologne and the departure to the United States in 1940 of my Uncle Gustav and his family. I knew that there were no graves for my aunt and uncle, and I felt that these stones bearing their names would prove to the world that they had not been forgotten.

In the meantime, Ibrahim had researched my story and noticed that the information I had written on the application for the Stolpersteine about my aunt and uncle's deportation was incorrect. For so many years I had thought they had been deported to Theresienstadt and Auschwitz. I learned only now that after they were forced to leave Marienburger Strasse they were sent to live in a Jewish house in Cologne and then deported to Riga in 1941, where they perished. Ibrahim also found their birth years. He advised us that the stones could be installed as early as April 2016, provided that sponsors could be found. It turned out that relatives were not supposed to pay for the Stolpersteine and now, more than seventy years after the end of World War II, unrelated people or companies had to be found that would pay for their installation. Much to our surprise, sponsors were located in no time, and the date for the installation in front of Marienburger Strasse 52 was set for April 12, 2016, at 11:20 a.m.

To my great regret, I was unable to join Marvin and his wife, Allegra, at the installation of the Stolpersteine. They later told me that the few hours they had spent in Cologne had been remarkable. It did not take long for the artist Gunter Demnig and his crew to fit the stones into the sidewalk outside the imposing house. The two sponsors had been present, as had the owner of the house and a journalist from a local news magazine. After two bouquets of flowers had been placed on either side of the stones, Marvin and Allegra had been invited to see the inside of the beautiful home surrounded by a lush garden. My fountain was long gone. The remainder of Marvin and Allegra's stay in Cologne had been spent in the company of one of the couples who had sponsored the installation.

Since my parents are buried in two different countries, these Stolpersteine are particularly meaningful for me. My father's grave is in the small Jewish cemetery on the outskirts of Oslo, Norway, and my mother's is in Montreal. Sadly, the cemetery in Oslo has been vandalized countless times. I have not visited my father's grave since 2002 and do not know its condition today. Now that the Stolpersteine carrying my parents' names are side by side, I feel that my parents are reunited.

~

When Stefan and I stood under the chuppah in the small synagogue in Oslo more than sixty-seven years ago, we could not have imagined the twists and turns our lives would have in store for us. Now that Stefan is ninety-four and I am eighty-eight years old, we often speak with wonderment about everything we have seen and done in our long lives.

I had thought in 2005 when I was writing this book that nothing worth mentioning would happen to me anymore, but I was wrong. In 2006, I was asked by the editors at Osprey Publishing in Oxford, England, to translate a Norwegian book originally written by the wife of a Norwegian Holocaust survivor and published in 1946. My English translation was published as *Counterfeiter: How a Norwegian Jew Survived the Holocaust*, and I was beyond excited when copies of the beautiful hardcover book were delivered to me in August 2008. That was the end of my translation career.

I also became a survivor speaker at the Montreal Holocaust Museum. I found my voice late in life, but after I got over my initial nervousness, I came to enjoy speaking to the young students who visit the museum. I have met many wonderful teachers and students and even received an award from the museum in September 2016.

In July 2013, Stefan and I moved to Westmount One, a home for seniors. Now that we have been living here for almost four years, Westmount One almost feels like home. We are able to lead the quiet and independent life we enjoy.

None of the above events can possibly compare with the growth spurt our family has undergone. Sara and Motti, who live in Beit Shemesh, Israel, are now the parents of eight, five boys and three girls. Shmoo married Raizel in Montreal in 2010, and they now have three boys and one girl, all also living in Beit Shemesh. Shooshoo married Roy in October 2010 in Israel, and they live in Petah Tikva with one daughter and two sons. Ashi married Dassy (Hadassah) in Israel in 2011, and they now live in Baltimore, Maryland, with their three boys. Since Dassy was born in Israel and has a large family there, Ashi and Dassy have one foot in Israel as well. Erin and her fiancé, Mike, are getting married in Toronto in June this year. Corinne and Yechiya have three daughters and live in Modi'in, Israel.

Our eighteen great-grandchildren are the legacy we are most proud of. Seventy-five years ago, Hitler and the Nazis vowed to annihilate the Jewish people, but our family is just one example that he did not succeed. To my great sorrow, antisemitism is raising its ugly head again in many places, including European countries, but based on past experience I feel sure that we will prevail.

My most fervent hope is for a safe and peaceful future for our family in Israel, the country they truly love.

Montreal, April 10, 2017

Glossary

aliyah (Hebrew; pl. *aliyot*, literally, ascent) A term used by Jews and modern Israelis to refer to Jewish immigration to Israel; the term is also used to refer to "going up" to the altar in a synagogue to read from the Torah.

Babi Yar A ravine on the northwest outskirts of Kiev, Ukraine. On September 29–30, 1941, Babi Yar was the site of one of the largest mass murders at an individual location during World War II, with over 33,000 Jews murdered by Nazi Einsatzgruppen mobile killing units (Russian estimates put the number at nearly 100,000). The ravine remained a site of murders of Jews, Roma, Soviet officials and prisoners of war through 1943.

bar mitzvah, bat mitzvah (Hebrew; literally, one to whom commandments apply) The age of thirteen when, according to Jewish tradition, boys become religiously and morally responsible for their actions and are considered adults for the purpose of synagogue ritual. A bar mitzvah is also the synagogue ceremony and family celebration that mark the attainment of this status, during which the boy is called upon to read a portion of the Torah and recite the prescribed prayers in a public prayer forum. In the latter half of the twentieth century, liberal Jews instituted an equivalent ceremony and celebration for girls called a bat mitzvah.

Bernadotte, Folke (1895–1948) A Swedish count and diplomat who, as vice-president of the Swedish Red Cross, is credited with convincing Heinrich Himmler in March and April 1945 to release 7,000 Scandinavian prisoners in German concentration camps, primarily from Sachsenhausen but also 400 Danish Jews in Theresienstadt. Bernadotte later arranged the release of 10,000 women prisoners from Ravensbrück concentration camp, including 2,000 Jews.

brit milah (Hebrew; in Yiddish, bris; literally, covenant of circumcision) Judaism's religious ceremony to welcome male infants into the covenant between God and the Children of Israel through a ritual circumcision (removal of the foreskin of the penis) performed by a mohel, or circumciser, eight days after the baby is born. Traditionally, a baby boy is named after this ceremony.

cheder (Hebrew; literally, room) An Orthodox Jewish elementary school that teaches the fundamentals of Jewish religious observance and textual study, as well as the Hebrew language.

chuppah (Hebrew; literally, covering) The canopy used in traditional Jewish weddings that is usually made of a cloth (sometimes a prayer shawl) stretched or supported over four poles. It is meant to symbolize the home the couple will build together.

Haftorah The portion read from the Book of Prophets after the Torah reading at Sabbath services and major festivals; it is traditionally sung by the youth who is celebrating his or her bar/bat mitzvah.

Haganah (Hebrew; The Defense) The Jewish paramilitary force in British Mandate Palestine that existed from 1920 to 1948 and later became the Israel Defense Forces. After World War II, there were branches of the Haganah in the DP camps in Europe, and members helped coordinate illegal immigration to British Mandate Palestine.

Hasidic Judaism (from the Hebrew word *hasid*; literally, piety) An Orthodox Jewish spiritual movement founded by Rabbi Israel ben Eliezer in eighteenth-century Poland; characterized by philosophies of mysticism and focusing on joyful prayer. This movement resulted in a new kind of leader who attracted disciples as opposed to the traditional rabbis who focused on the intellectual study of Jewish law. Melody and dance have an important role in Hasidic worship. There are many different sects of Hasidic Judaism, but followers of Hasidism often wear dark, conservative clothes as well as a head covering to reflect modesty and show respect to God.

Jewish houses (In German, *Judenhäuser*) Designated areas or buildings in German cities where German Jews were forced to live, beginning as early as May 1939. These residences were crowded, cramped apartments or even shared rooms. While living in these spaces, Jews often were required to perform compulsory forced labour before eventually being deported to concentration or death camps. These Jewish houses were found only in German cities and differed from the ghettos constructed elsewhere in Nazi-occupied Europe, which were areas of the city in which Jews were more strictly confined.

kibbutz (Hebrew) A collectively owned farm or settlement in Israel, democratically governed by its members.

Kristallnacht (German; literally, Night of Broken Glass) A series of pogroms that took place in Germany and Austria between November 9 and 10, 1938. Over the course of twenty-four hours, ninety-one Jews were murdered, 25,000–30,000 were arrested and deported to concentration camps, two hundred synagogues were destroyed and thousands of Jewish businesses and homes were ransacked. Planned by the Nazis as a coordinated attack on the Jews of Germany and Austria, Kristallnacht is often seen as an important turning point in Hitler's policies of systematic persecution of Jews.

Little Norway A training base in Toronto, Canada, near the Toronto Island Airport for exiled Norwegian airmen and soldiers during World War II.

March of the Living An annual event that was established in 1988 and takes place in April on Holocaust Memorial Day (Yom Hashoah) in Poland. The March of the Living program aims to educate primarily Jewish students and young adults from around the world about the Holocaust and Jewish life during World War II. Along with Holocaust survivors, participants march the three kilometres from Auschwitz to Birkenau to commemorate all who perished in the Holocaust. The concept of the event comes from the Nazi death marches that Jews were forced to go on when they were being evacuated from the forced labour and concentration camps at the very end of the war. Many Jews died during these marches and the March of the Living was thus created both to remember this history and to serve as a contrast to it by celebrating Jewish life and strength. After spending time in Poland, participants travel to Israel and join in celebrations there for Israel's remembrance and independence days.

Organization for Rehabilitation through Training (ORT) A vocational school system founded for Jews by Jews in Russia in 1880. The name ORT derives from the acronym of the Russian organization *Obshestvo Remeslenogo Zemledelcheskogo Truda*, Society for Trades and Agricultural Labour.

Pesach (Hebrew; also, Passover) One of the major festivals of the Jewish calendar, Passover takes place over eight days in the spring. One of the main observances of the holiday is to recount the story of Exodus, the Jews' flight from slavery in Egypt, at a ritual meal called a seder. The name itself refers to the fact that God "passed over" the houses of the Jews when he set about slaying the firstborn sons of Egypt as the last of the ten plagues aimed at convincing Pharaoh to free the Jews.

Riga The capital city of Latvia. Before World War II, from 1918 to 1940, Riga was the capital of independent Latvia. After being annexed by the Soviets in August 1940, Riga was occupied by Nazi Germany in July 1941. Twenty thousand Jews were deported to the closed ghetto in Riga from Germany and other occupied areas. By the time the Soviet army liberated Riga on October 13, 1944, nearly all the Jews in Riga had been murdered by the Nazis.

Righteous Among the Nations A title bestowed by Yad Vashem, the Holocaust Martyrs' and Heroes' Remembrance Authority in Jerusalem, to honour non-Jews who risked their lives to help save Jews during the Holocaust. A commission was established in 1963 to award the title. If a person fits certain criteria and the story is carefully corroborated, the honouree is awarded with a medal and certificate and commemorated on the Wall of Honour at the Garden of the Righteous in Jerusalem.

seder (Hebrew; literally, order) A ritual family meal celebrated at the beginning of the festival of Passover.

Six-Day War The armed conflict between Israel and the neighbouring states of Egypt, Jordan and Syria that took place from June 5–10, 1967. In response to Egypt closing the Straits of Tiran to Israeli shipping, the creation of an alliance between Egypt, Syria and Jordan, and the mobilization of troops by Egypt's leader Gamal Nasser along Israel's borders, Israel launched a pre-emptive attack. In the days that followed, Israeli forces drove the armies back and occupied the Sinai Peninsula, Gaza Strip, West Bank and Golan Heights. Israel also reunited Jerusalem, the eastern half of which Jordan had controlled since the 1948–1949 war.

Theresienstadt A walled town in the Czech Republic sixty kilometres north of Prague that served as both a ghetto and a concentration camp. More than 73,000 Jews from the German Protectorate of Bohemia and Moravia and from the Greater German Reich (including Austria and parts of Poland) were deported to Theresienstadt between 1941 and 1945, 60,000 of whom were deported to Auschwitz or other death camps. Theresienstadt was showcased as a "model" ghetto for propaganda purposes to demonstrate to delegates from the International Red Cross and others the "humane" treatment of Jews and to counter information reaching the

Allies about Nazi atrocities and mass murder. Theresienstadt was liberated on May 8, 1945, by the Soviet Red Army.

ulpan (Hebrew; pl. *ulpanim*) A school that offers an intensive Hebrew-language study program. *Ulpanim*, the first of which was established in Jerusalem in 1949, were created to help new immigrants learn the language of their new country and acclimatize to its culture.

Women's International Zionist Organization (w i z o) An organization founded in England in 1920 to help women and children in what was then British Mandate Palestine and is now Israel. w i z o is currently the largest women's Zionist organization in the world.

Yad Vashem The Holocaust Martyrs' and Heroes' Remembrance Authority, established in 1953 to commemorate, educate the public about, research and document the Holocaust.

yeshiva (Hebrew) A Jewish educational institution in which religious texts such as the Torah and Talmud are studied.

Zionism A movement promoted by the Viennese Jewish journalist Theodor Herzl, who argued in his 1896 book *Der Judenstaat* (The Jewish State) that the best way to resolve the problem of antisemitism and persecution of Jews in Europe was to create an independent Jewish state in the historic Jewish homeland of Biblical Israel. Zionists also promoted the revival of Hebrew as a Jewish national language.

Photographs

Margrit (left) with her friend Marta. Buahaugen, Norway, 1941.

1 Margrit's father's family. From left to right: Margit's Aunt Karolienchen; her grandparents, Veilchen and Jakob; Aunt Selma; Uncle Gustav; and Uncle Natan. Wächtersbach, Germany, 1920s.

2 Margrit's father, Max (Markus) Rosenberg, with his dog. Cologne, Germany. Circa 1935.

3 Margrit and her father, Max (Markus) Rosenberg. Circa 1947.

Margrit and her husband, Stefan, in Norway before immigrating to Canada. 1951.

Margrit (right) with her mother, Alice, at her daughter's wedding. July 12, 1981.

The Wellén cottage at Buahaugen, Norway. This cottage is similar to the one Margrit's family escaped to during the war, which was burned down during a German raid after her family left for Sweden. 1996.

1

2

1   Einar Wellén (left) and Margrit's son, Marvin, (right), standing in front of Stefan
and Margrit at the Granlis' house in Rogne, Norway, where Margrit lived with her
family during the war. 1996.

2   From left to right: Stefan, Margrit and their son, Marvin. The Granlis' house in
Rogne, Norway, 1996.

1 Israeli ambassador Michael Shiloh (left) with Einar Wellén (right) at the ceremo-
   ny honouring Einar as Righteous Among the Nations by Yad Vashem for saving
   Margrit and her family. Oslo, Norway, April 16, 1996.
2 Reception at the Wellén home after the ceremony honouring Einar as Righteous
   Among the Nations. Margrit is seated next to Einar; others are unknown. Oslo,
   Norway, April 1996.

Margrit's daughter, Helen, relaxing from her hectic schedule, circa 2015.

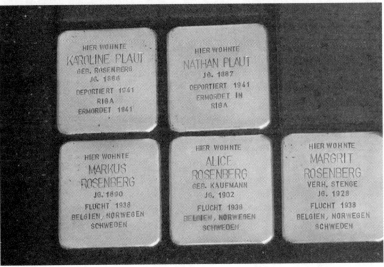

1 Margrit's childhood home at Marienburger Strasse 52. Cologne, Germany. Photo circa 2016.

2 The Stolpersteine commemorating Margrit's family at Marienburger Strasse 52 in Cologne, Germany. The Stolpersteine include the dates of deportation or escape from Germany. Top, from left to right: Margrit's Aunt Karolienchen (Karoline) Plaut and her Uncle Natan (Nathan) Plaut, deported in 1941. Bottom, from left to right: Margrit's father, Max (Markus) Rosenberg, her mother, Alice Rosenberg, and Margrit, escaped in 1938. April 12, 2016.

Index

Fondation
Azrieli
Foundation

The Azrieli Foundation was established in 1989 to realize and extend the philanthropic vision of David J. Azrieli, C.M., C.Q., M.Arch. The Foundation's mission is to support a wide spectrum of initiatives in education and research. The Azrieli Foundation is an active supporter of programs in the fields of education, the education of architects, scientific and medical research, and the arts. The Azrieli Foundation's many initiatives include: the Holocaust Survivor Memoirs Program, which collects, preserves, publishes and distributes the written memoirs of survivors in Canada; the Azrieli Institute for Educational Empowerment, an innovative program successfully working to keep at-risk youth in school; the Azrieli Fellows Program, which promotes academic excellence and leadership on the graduate level at Israeli universities; the Azrieli Music Project, which celebrates and fosters the creation of high-quality new Jewish orchestral music; and the Azrieli Neurodevelopmental Research Program, which supports advanced research on neurodevelopmental disorders, particularly Fragile X and Autism Spectrum Disorders.